To my dearest most special friend,
for all the years past, and all the years to come
my love and friendship
Julie xx

COLOUR YOUR HOME

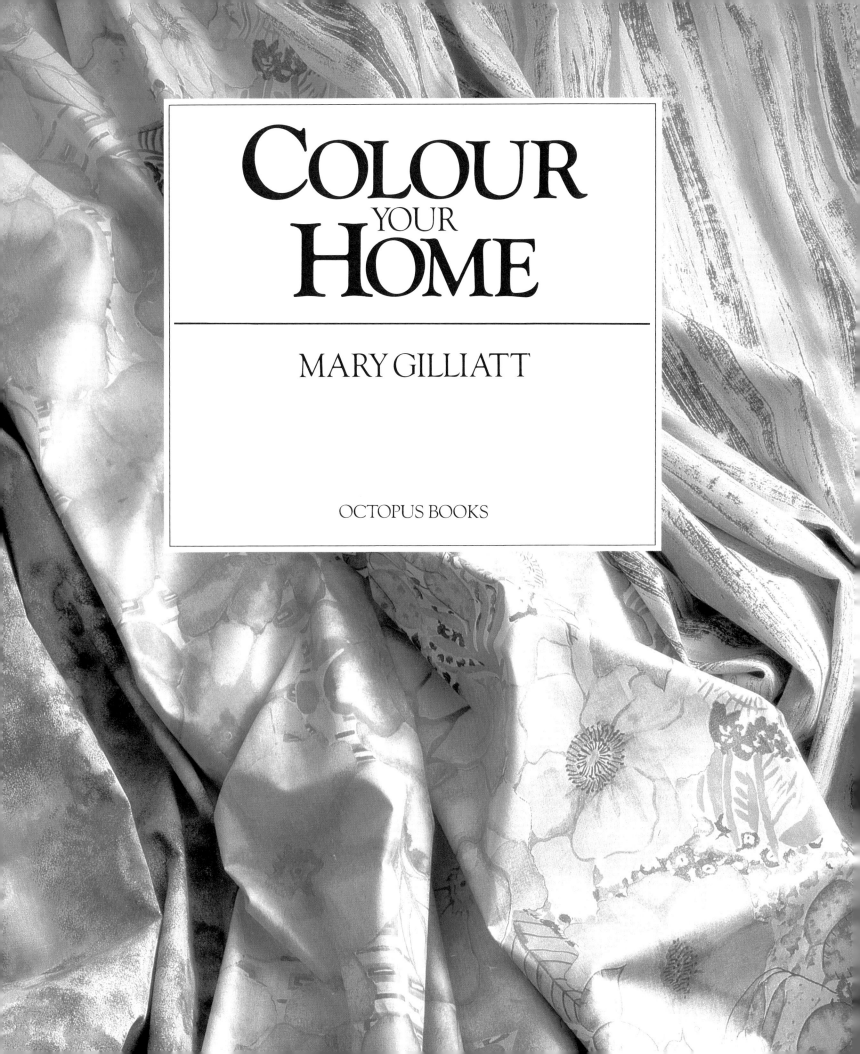

COLOUR
YOUR
HOME

MARY GILLIATT

OCTOPUS BOOKS

Author's Acknowledgements
Many people helped in the production of this book and I am most grateful to them all. But I would like to record my particular appreciation to Marita Byrne and Vanessa Pryse of Octopus, who conceived and planned the whole production and carried it out with good-humoured perseverance; to Nadine Bazar, who researched all the pictures and to Charlie Stebbings, who photographed the still lifes. I also want to give so many thanks to my loyal, cheerful, and hardworking assistants: Sarah Allen, who did the research; and Annabel Longworth, who did all the leg work. And finally, as always, I have to thank my patient family and friends for putting up with my peripatetic life.

First published 1985 by
Octopus Books Limited
59 Grosvenor Street
London W1

© Octopus Books Limited 1985

ISBN 0 7064 2343 7

Produced by Mandarin Publishers Limited
22a Westlands Road
Quarry Bay, Hong Kong

Printed in Hong Kong

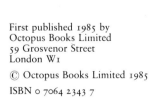

CONTENTS

INTRODUCTION

Colour is the most malleable, the most exciting, the most immediately noticeable and the least expensive element in decorating. Different combinations of colours can make the same room seem welcoming or impersonal, warm or cool, restful or stimulating, harmonious or jarring. Moreover, the choice of colours we make when decorating is both central to our own moods and to the impression our home will make on other people.

In short, colour is extremely important in decoration, but the trouble is that a very great number of people have a hard time developing the confidence to use it properly. I am particularly aware of this because I conduct a series of design seminars or clinics in both the United States and Britain, and the questions I get asked over and over are invariably about colour schemes, where to get started and how.

Some rare individuals can carry a colour around in their heads and match it absolutely. They look at a room and know instantly what will suit it. Most of us, however, have to work at developing colour sense, and the way to do so is really to look at any pleasurable combinations we see and to analyze the make-up of colours within that image in a conscious way.

For a start, almost anything that pleases you visually can be converted into the basis of a

decorative scheme if you keep the colours in just about the same proportions and translate them into carpet, walls, window treatments and accessories. Most rural scenes, for example, contain innumerable shades of green, harmoniously blended with accents provided by bright splashes of colour from flowers, berries or crops. Similarly, an old-fashioned rose garden can show how to make successful blends of pinks, yellows and peaches, creating a scheme of equal tones against a green background. Or take the build-up of colours in any Mediterranean village.

The Impressionists, particularly Vincent Van Gogh, have much to teach us about observing colour. They developed the habit of almost always describing everything they saw in the minutest breakdown of tones and shades. Van Gogh's letters are full of descriptions. For example, in a letter to John Russell, an Australian painter, he wrote of a picture by Monet ' . . . a landscape with red sunset and a group of dark fir trees by the sea side. The red sun casts an orange or blood-red reflection on the blue trees and the ground. I wish I could see them'.

Interestingly, Van Gogh and his fellow Impressionists had been deeply influenced by the theories of a Monsieur M.E. Chevreul, manager of the great Gobelins tapestry factory in France. Chevreul had observed that two differently coloured threads appeared to have a single colour when seen from a distance. Following on from this discovery, he delved into the whole theory of colour and eventually wrote The Principles of Harmony and Contrast of Colours, which has remained a leading textbook on the subject ever since.

In this book, I have tried to put Chevreul's principles into practice by first discussing each colour in an emotive way, conjuring up and analyzing the visions that a particular colour evokes. Then I have divided that colour into all its various shades, discussing which other colours best complement them, when and how the colour can be used as an accent or be accented, and, finally, how it goes with equal tones – dark, bright, pastel and so on – of other colours. In his work, Chevreul notes that once certain rules have been absorbed, painters use colours to better effect, and I must say just from writing this particular book I have learnt to look at scenes with his rulings in mind and to appreciate how right he is. The rules which apply to painting should be just as true of decoration, as this book sets out to show.

SHADES AND CONTRASTS

The glowing autumnal colours of a forest with the soft sunlight filtering through the sparse foliage are so rich, yet serene, that they seem ideal for the purposes of interior design. The shades of golden yellows and browns of the leaves, the muted greens of the grass and shrubs, and the mauve light in the distance blend harmoniously and are contrasted by the dark, greenish-grey trunks. It is easy to imagine these colours translated into floors, walls and soft furnishings. Whatever the composition, the result is certain to be warm and inviting.

ACCENT

A sunny cornfield gently moving in the wind is evocative of peace and tranquility as well as being pleasing to the eye. The appearance of a bright scarlet poppy, the ultimate accent, makes the scene zing with life. In much the same way a vase full of red tulips in a predominantly green room would invigorate the whole scheme. The same effect could be created with a red print or *objet d'art*, or with red piping on a sofa. Because red is such a strong, dominant colour, it acts particularly well as an accent in schemes that are in themselves more restful.

EQUAL TONES

A beautiful sunny beach on a tropical island brings to mind a very different juxtaposition of colours compared to those of a more northern landscape. Here, the bleached sand, the turquoise water and the blue sky are all in perfect harmony, none being more dominant than the others in terms of setting the scene. The palm trees add life and interest to the whole in much the same way as a foliage plant would indoors. The picture conjures up visions of a modern clean-lined interior, where pattern is kept to a minimum and the interaction of the colours is the main theme: a potentially striking scheme.

YELLOW

BRIGHT, HAPPY, SUNNY, WARM,
GLOWING, LIVELY

Yellow is the colour of sunlight, gold, sandy beaches, spring flowers and the dazzle of buttercups and dandelions in summer meadows. Equally, it is the colour of glowing fires, autumn sunsets and lighted windows at night; of crysanthemums, apples and pears and fallen leaves. It is associated with brightness and cheerfulness, warmth and sparkle, although, paradoxically, it is also associated with cowardice and sickliness, with the cold clear moon and the remote gleam of the stars. It begins subtly with palest primrose, blonde hair and hay, and ends with the richness of amber, the glow of apricots and the deep tawny ochre of burnt Sienna.

Yellow has been used in decoration and in clothes from the earliest times. The Egyptians made a bright yellow from orpiment, a mineral found in their soil, and it was they who first developed the technique of gilding.

The Romans used the orange-yellow dye saffron, made from the stigma of the autumnal crocus, for their robes, particularly at marriage ceremonies, where the bride traditionally wore an orange veil and shoes.

In medieval times, painters used a brownish-yellow pigment called ochre to deepen other colours. Sienna, an orange-yellow earth pigment containing iron oxide and named after the

Italian city of Sienna, was another important component of the medieval painter's palette.

The Italian earthenware called maiolica, very popular in the Renaissance period, used deep ochre and bright clear yellows in the biblical or allegorical scenes with which it was painted.

Apricot was an immensely fashionable colour in the eighteenth century, brought back to Britain by young aristocrats who had completed their education by making the Grand Tour of Europe, especially if they had extended their travels into India.

The lighter yellows and pastel shades tend to look somewhat washed-out under a hot southern sun, and it is in the more temperate climates that these shades come into their own, whether the bright, clear yellow silks which were fashionable for upholstery and furnishing in the Regency period in Britain or the pale yellows used by English water-colourists.

Yellow is, of course, a primary colour, along with blue and red which combine to produce purple, the complementary colour to yellow. Like red and orange, it has the effect of advancing surfaces, bringing them closer to the eye. Yellow and orange lie next to each other in the colour wheel and should not be used in equal quantities in a decorative scheme or they will cancel each other out.

SHADES AND CONTRASTS

The liveliness of the yellows range from butter to tangerine, blonde hair to saffron, primrose to chrysanthemums. Here, the warm soft yellow of the wallpaper, an instantly cheerful and cheering sunlight colour, is echoed in the cream, pale lemon and peach of the fabric and contrasted quietly by the muted green and more strongly by the bright white. The juxtaposition gives an immediate impression of what a room in these colours would look like: warm and happy, but with a freshness provided by the green and the white. Here are colours which gleam in a sunny room or add warmth to a north-facing setting.

ACCENT

Yellow accents are instant fresheners, revivers, sharpeners: the zing of lemon; the lift to the spirit at the sight of a yellow sou'wester on a grey and rainy day, or yellow crocuses pushing up through cold, wet grass. In decorating terms, it hardly matters whether the accent is a bunch of flowers, the yellow in a painting or in part of a pattern; the point is that the kind of light given out by even the palest yellow provides a liveliness and focus in just about any kind of space or room scheme you care to think of. Here, yellow is the only colour in an all-white room, where texture has also been used to add interest.

EQUAL TONES

Whether yellow is used as a pale pastel or in much richer, sharper or darker shades, it equalizes well with other colours in the same tones. Here it is used with blues and holds its own with a certain amount of vigour, as in the natural spring combinations of daffodils and grape hyacinths. The result is fresh and cheerful and would look good in any room, due to the natural balance created by using yellow, an advancing colour, with cool, recessive blue. In a sun-drenched room, the blue would add a welcome hint of coolness, while the yellow would have the reverse effect on a cold room.

SHADES AND CONTRASTS

In nature, yellow is often found as a background colour: a yellowish dusty road, for instance, or a mellow ochre stone wall. If you are planning a room with a predominantly yellow theme, it helps to recall a scene from nature in which your chosen yellow predominates and then the other colours which either contrast or harmonize with this shade will also come to mind.

For instance, build up an image in your mind's eye, as accurate as you can make it, of a field of ripe corn, complete with patches of scorched earth and the splashes of colour created by scarlet poppies among the burnished gold, the edging of grass and the varying greens of the trees, or the hedges studied with the pink of wild roses. All this would suggest a burnt Sienna or soft earth-coloured carpet, with walls the colour of corn and green or green and yellow curtains. The upholstery would be in contrasting green and deeper yellow, with cushions in red or pink or both.

Alternatively, examine a honeysuckle flower and see how the yellow dissolves into a rich cream with tinges of rose or apricot. This could inspire pale yellow walls tinted with apricot or peach, a soft terracotta and cream carpet (since honeysuckle so often climbs against old brick), and seating in the fresh greens of honeysuckle leaves and in the creams and peaches of the petals, with curtains and blinds of much the same colouring.

Another theme might be an old-fashioned shrub-rose garden, with its multi-coloured petals of yellow, apricot,

pink, red and white, its grassy border and patches of earth. This could be translated in terms of a soft brown or green carpet and yellow or yellow and rose walls, with yellow, rose, cream and white fabrics.

Or take the colours of a sunset: yellow, rose, apricot and lilac fading into blue grey, and relate them to a polished floor with a dhurrie rug of yellow and faded blue and rose, pale yellow walls and slightly brighter curtains, with rose, apricot and grey upholstery.

On another tack, you could think of a beach: fine yellow sand contrasting with the blue green of the water and the clear blue sky, and with reddish or ochre rocks standing out against white sails and clouds. Here you could use a sand-coloured carpet with bluey-green or sky blue walls and touches of ochre, terracotta or white. Or reverse the process and have an aquamarine carpet with sand walls and sand and terracotta fabric. You might, indeed, think of dark pines, sand and water, and produce a sand-coloured carpet with dark green walls, contrasts of aqua, and the sort of faded rose red to be seen on boats and deck chairs.

ABOVE Patterned wallpaper in primrose yellow scattered with deep pink roses contrasts with white woodwork and dark mahogany in this cheerful space. A darker shade of yellow backs the shelving to create a sense of perspective and depth and the mirror above the table has a similar effect, preventing the yellow and rose from becoming claustrophobic. Note how the mahogany and the green leaves, edged with yellow, of the plant provide a gentle contrast to the background in much the same way as the browns and yellows of a hedgerow stand out against a field of ripening wheat or barley.

RIGHT Here, brilliant yellow walls form a vibrant contrast to the stunning collection of blue and white china on the old white-painted mantelpiece. The painted chest adds both a sophisticated and a cooling edge to the warm and otherwise casual country room, and the matting on the floor, edging into the baskets, which in turn edge into the curtain fabric, gives a nice sense of balance to the predominant yellow.

ABOVE Simple yellow lampshades crowning slender wooden bases are part of a gentle build-up of colour in a harmonious yellow still life. The arrangement of dried flowers and herbs runs the gamut of shades from palest straw through marmalade to ochre, and its cane basket container is nicely balanced on one side by the slightly yellowing photograph and the group of small boxes and on the other by the wooden decoy duck. The general effect is lively, with the monochromatic scheme giving an underlying unity to a collection of objects which might otherwise appear somewhat overcrowded.

LEFT Creamy yellow walls, ceiling and curtains are balanced in this casual room by cane chairs with cream cotton cushions, pinky cream cotton sofas and a warm beige carpet, and contrasted with airy festoon blinds (shades) in deep apricot. The green of plants in this creamy composition stands out in an interestingly three-dimensional way, providing touches of living colour against the gentle, muted background.

ABOVE Chinz-covered sofas in shades of apricot, yellow and pink, with contrasts of sludgy green, work well with the warm sandy walls, the painting, plants and bunch of hydrangeas. White curtains and fireplace add just the requisite amount of freshness. This sort of scheme works as well in winter, when the warm colours provide a pleasant contrast to the starkness outside and the flickering flames of the fire add yet more touches of yellow and orange, as it does in summer, when it seems almost like an extension of the garden.

LEFT Green and apricot stencilling in the thirties' manner gives interesting detailing to otherwise plain daffodil yellow walls. The same feeling is repeated with the bunch of yellow tulips in their shaded yellow to green vase. Note how their fanned-out shape is repeated in the shape of the floor lamp just above them, which reflects the overall yellowness, as do the golden tones of the wood cabinet and the sepia of the picture. The effect is to turn a dark corner into a space glowing with colour.

RIGHT This whole room is a composition of warm yellows layered one upon another, repeating shades upon shades, contrast with contrast. The large painted oak leaves on the walls repeat the burnt orange and celadon green of the vase on the mantelshelf, the painting, and the dried flowers in the green glass. The same autumnal colours are repeated again in the painted closets with their darker stippled frames; in the throw draped languidly over the chair (though here they are sharpened somewhat and accented with blue); in the fireplace tiles, and even in the fire itself. The slightly paler green paint above the dragged ochre picture rail is again echoed in the painting, and, along with the grey white of the marble mantelpiece, cools the whole.

ACCENT

Yellow is a particularly good accent colour, brightening and illuminating almost any colour you care to mention, from whites, neutrals and tawny browns, to blacks, the full range of blues, rose pinks and reds.

For example, study a bee or wasp, with the accenting of the yellow stripe against the deep brown. A tobacco-coloured room with darker upholstery could display saffron-coloured cushions to good effect, and perhaps a golden Afghan rug.

Remember the yellow streaks against the rich purple blue of irises and the bright yellow pollen which contrasts so vividly with the delicate petals of the violet. This could inspire yellow walls, softly structured blue blinds, a blue carpet, deeper blue upholstery and yellow cushions or flowers or both.

Yellow stamens, of course, accent the colour of any petals, particularly white ones: the phrase 'fresh as a daisy' is a very apt description of the startlingly pristine air of a single daisy, with its intense yellow centre. Repeat the look with an all-white room, spiced with brilliant yellow cushions and flowers, or perhaps a painting or prints mounted on yellow matts or a yellow border round the wall or edging the curtain fabric. Choose yellow and white tiles for a kitchen or bathroom, and set yellow tiles against white walls in any house in the sun.

Many people choose a neutral background colouring because they find grey, beiges, creams and buffs quite the most restful colours to live with and the best backdrop for clothes. Equally, they may well feel safer with neutrals because they think that it is difficult to make a mistake with such subtle colouring.

However, unless used with artistic sense and a deft touch, neutrals can be restful to the point of monotony. To avoid this, add a splash of yellow or orange here and there and the scheme will come to life immediately. The great artist-gardener Gertrude Jekyll, writing at the turn of the century, noted how her grey garden, in which all the plants had either grey or silver leaves, was best approached through the orange borders: 'the effect is . . . luminous and refreshing'. Similarly, pale grey walls and upholstery will look marvellously fresh with a yellow, white and grey carpet or rug. Beautiful buffs and beiges zing with a vase of creamy yellow roses, a bunch of mimosa, a jug of crysanthemums, or a glimpse of a yellow lining to a curtain. And try edging the walls just below the ceiling with a thin line of brass or gilded strips of wood. The gleam of yellow will give just that extra touch of luxury.

LEFT A simple bunch of bright yellow daffodils adds life and interest to this traditional-looking bedroom, where walls, curtains and bedspread are all in varying shades of white. The only other contrasts are provided by the brass at the top of the bedhead and the pine bedside table. It is interesting to note how different types of lace have been used to create depth. The result is restful but fresh, reminiscent of a white daisy with yellow stamen.

RIGHT Yellow is the instant livening accent in this spare, cool, basically bluish-grey and white bedroom. Touches of yellow at the base of the green fronds and in the geometric design of the bedspread, together with the merest hint of it in the off-white of the walls and the bleached wood of the floor is enough to breathe life and liveliness into the whole.

EQUAL TONES

Equal tones used in the right proportion to one another make a room particularly restful. In order to achieve the peace and calm which are engendered by a harmonious palette of colours, no single colour should be brighter or harder than any other, and no colour should jar or seem out of context.

If you are at a loss to think of such colour juxtapositions, examine paintings by acknowledged masters of harmony: a Dutch interior by Vermeer, perhaps, with its characteristic blend of rich yet soft yellow, blue and grey; or the gentle pastel tones of George Seurat in which the luminous effect is created by dancing dots of yellow along with the other clear colours which build up the image, or the luxurious clothing in a painting by the Venetian master, Titian.

Apricot, grey and dove blue, or soft lemon yellow, pale grey and powder blue are two groups which harmonize particularly well. Alternatively, you could think in terms of landscape, conjuring up the bright green and yellow of a meadow of buttercups or the green, blue and yellow of a wood carpeted with bluebells and daffodils. Whether you think directly of the various colour combinations or borrow a scheme from nature, the images evoked should suggest good room schemes.

In the pastel range, a white room looks agreeably fresh with upholstery in pale yellow and pink, pistachio green or soft sky blue, or a combination of all these pastels in well-designed prints. Another option is to use pale blue or pink and yellow throughout a room, with touches of green or of pearl grey, lemon yellow and soft white.

Apricots marry particularly well with soft, clear greens and blues or with nutmeg browns and blues. Just think of a ripe apricot fringed with leaves and silhouetted against a summer sky or trained against an old wall. The warm rosy glow of a flawless apricot skin, incidentally, is best created with yellow overpainted or rag-rubbed with rose paint, which will give a much truer feeling of apricot than any solidly painted wall could do.

The washed yellows and terracottas and faded greens of Mediterranean countries under cloudless blue skies harmonize as well in interiors as they do in villages climbing up mountain sides.

Really, all you need to do is to analyze any vignette that seems especially agreeable and peaceful to you: separate out the colours, think about their proportions one with another, and you will be furnished with a dozen different schemes with which to work.

ABOVE Van Gogh, one feels, would have happily set up this simple still life for yet another variation on his beloved yellow theme: yellow tulips tinged with pink, russet and green apples, the terracotta of the bowl and the stronger splashes of colour in the jug; sandy yellow stripes on the tablecloth verging into the pink and blue; the green which merges into the green leaves, and all in harmony with the honey of chairs, table and wallpaper.

LEFT Equal tones of yellow, pink, lilac and green all merge together against a white background in this small airy bedroom. The paper border used as a dado rail all round the room echoes the colours of the framed poster above the bed. The striped bathrobe over the chair is half wall/half floor colour and the neatly piled boxes on the high yellow-edged shelf repeat the room's tones over again. The colours are as gentle as the soft pink and yellow of an old rose garden with patches of blue sky above.

LEFT The strong vibrant geometric designs of the fabrics dominate this cheerful room: the glowing colours of the curtains are repeated in the sofa and cushions, but the design is simpler and more restful. These vivid co-ordinating fabrics use primary and secondary colours in equal proportions. In conjunction with saffron yellow walls, they bring all the warmth of a herbaceous border, a bunch of polyanthus, or the Caribbean (depending on your imagery) to a winter room. But note the balance of colours: the way the reds and yellows and pinks are cooled by the greens and blues and white.

ABOVE A sensuously squashy chrome yellow sofa is the focal point in a spare white country room – that, and the interesting yellow reflections on the wall of windows at the far end. The pair of dove grey cushions (pillows) subtly reflects the colours of the appliqué picture, and adds a touch of sobriety while the yellow and white lilies echo the general composition. Nevertheless, it is yellow that really sets the tone in a room which might have looked cold and uninviting in a less vibrant colour scheme.

GREEN

RESTFUL, FRESH, COOL, SOOTHING,
NATURAL, INFORMAL

*Green is a natural and emotive colour, conjuring
up the pleasures of sheltering trees, dappled
meadows, blue-green hills and fresh young
leaves. There is the sombre green of conifers, the
shining Christmas colour of holly and ivy, the
aqueous light of caves, the damp tender shade
of moss and lichen, the velvety splendour of a
well-kept lawn. And there is the lovely juxtaposition of silvery-green willow branches
drooping languidly into sun-dappled green-
brown water.*

*Rarely, for a colour, green also conjures up
smells along with vision: the sweetness of new-
mown grass, the intoxicating freshness of leaves
after rain or the invigorating scent of wet pine
needles luxuriously translated into a hot bath.*

*Natural greens range from the merest tinge of
colour in Christmas roses and apple flesh to the
dark blue green of Douglas firs, with a gamut of
green herbs, vegetables and insects in between.
There is also one of the most precious stones,
the emerald, as well as the semi-precious
Chinese jade, the coppery green of malachite so
beloved of the Russian Czars, the light clear
tone of semi-precious peridot and the heavy
green glass of wine bottles.*

*Various shades of green have gone in and out
of fashion over the centuries. The Georgians
imported the bright apple green from France*

which was to be a favourite colour until later in the eighteenth century, when it gave way to the paler green of Robert Adam. Adam had been inspired by the beautiful celadon vases produced by the Chinese during the Sung dynasty (AD 960–1279), the glaze of which ranged from cool blue greens to greyish olive. He used cool greens and blues, offset by white and by pastel pink, to create the 'noble splendour' and 'calm grandeur' of the neo-classical era.

During both the first and second Napoleonic empires, the French favoured their emerald green, also known as empire green.

In mid-Victorian Britain there was a passion for dull dark greens, inspired by the Aesthetic movement, which set the fashion for 'greenery yallery'. These colours were much used by William Morris in his textiles and wallpapers. A lustier deep forest green was favoured for walls in the 1930s.

Green is technically a secondary colour since it is a mixture of blue and yellow and comes between them in the spectrum. Its complementary colour is red and it is analogous with blue, so equal amounts of either of these with green will only serve to cancel both colours out. It is a receding colour and is generally known as a cool one though, paradoxically, dark greens can seem very warm.

SHADES AND CONTRASTS

Green, like blue, is one of the predominant colours of nature. Practically any shade of green contrasts well with almost any shade of blue and in this particular fabric the wide range of greens is also contrasted with red, pink and warm yellow – a soft fruit collection of colours. The wallpaper is a subtle green on green, an emulation of a paint technique. This mixture of greens is restful yet interesting, while the contrasting colours add warmth and liveliness. So much green might have too much of a cooling, recessive influence on a large, north-facing room, but it could create a calm, restful atmosphere in a very bright situation.

ACCENT

The easiest green accent to add to a room has to be any sort of green plant. Whatever the predominant colour or style of the setting, the freshness of leaves adds a new dimension and depth, creating an oasis of coolness in, for example, a basically red or yellow room. But any touch of green, such as the pastel green which defines the floral pattern of the fabric, will act as a coolant when added to a warm room. On the other hand, green is rarely cold – it is too inherently relaxing and peaceful to have this effect – and in this scene the green touches in the warm fabric and the plant offset the white of the curtain, walls and floor.

EQUAL TONES

Green is the great equalizer, as much indoors as it is outside, and since it is such a predominant background colour to life in general, it holds its own with the three primaries – red, yellow and blue – despite being technically classed as a secondary colour. Here, a bright vivid green holds its own with strong primary colours against a white background in this matching fabric and wallpaper. The brilliant white emphasizes the brightness and cheerfulness of the other colours which, combined with the simple, uncomplicated design, create a scheme which would be ideal for a child's room.

SHADES AND CONTRASTS

Because green is the overriding colour of nature, painters have always been fascinated by the exercise of recreating its subtleties and moods. Constable, that most lyrical of landscape painters, is well worth detailed observation. Delacroix, the great French artist, recalled in his journal: 'Constable says that the superiority of greens in his meadows is due to the fact that they are made up of a large number of different (juxtaposed, not mixed) greens.'

The same principle can be applied to rooms, where a mixture of greens gives a much more natural, living feel to a scheme than any single green used throughout. In a sun-dappled water meadow, for example, you would find yellowy greens, grey greens, sludgy brown greens, reddish green and almost certainly the contrast of a white gate (or Constable's white-painted Flatford Mill), the browny grey of an old wood fence, a flash of red in a poppy or the yellow of a buttercup. All these colours would translate easily into wall colours and soft furnishings.

Much the same sort of inspiration could be received by studying the contrasts shown in the exuberant, exotic jungle of the brilliant primitive painter Henri Rousseau, with its mixture of dark and vivid greens and bright contrasting yellows, or the sensual serenity of Monet's water lily ponds. To reproduce the atmosphere of the former, exuberant prints could be offset by two-toned green-striped walls, while a room influenced by Monet might have a

gentler, paint-effect background and, for example, fabrics in green and rose.

The blue green of the sea with the ochre and rose of shore and rocks can be translated by upholstery and curtains in the same colours against ochre and rose rag-rubbed walls. Again, the interpretation could be in darker shades of greeny blue and rose terracotta, with touches of deep green and red, or in clearer shades of limpid sea green and brighter ochre with touches of blue and red, depending on one's personal vision of the sea under differing lights and weathers.

On a different tack, a bowling or cricket match could act as an inspiration: the vivid green of the close-mown grass, the creamy white of the players' clothes, the brilliant colours of the balls and the blurred patchwork of spectators could all be translated into wall and floor coverings, plain fabrics and prints.

LEFT The soft, variegated greens of the fabrics in this pleasant room are reminiscent of the limpid look of a dense tangle of willows along a river bank. The juxtaposed greens give a most interesting 'living' feel to the space, the sort of liveliness and depth which could never have been achieved by a series of solid colours. The effect is serene, sunny and very comfortable.

ABOVE The pale and dark greens, apricots and yellows of the printed fabric on this sofa are well complemented by the subtle sage greens of the walls and woodwork, the soft olive of the table and the grey green of the floor. The juxtaposition of the strong design, with its rose pink throw, is pleasingly complemented by the much more delicate pattern of the window blinds (shades) in much the same colours but used in quite different weights, the earthenware vase of massed flowers, the group of wooden candlesticks and matching wooden bowl, and the punch of the fresh green tracery of leaves, balanced by the bright green apples in the pink ceramic bowl. Again, the range of variegated greens, although allied this time to the colours of a rose garden, make a most restful and inviting room.

ABOVE Fresh green-sprigged paper co-ordinates with an equally fresh green and white window fabric and a beautifully painted corner cabinet to make a beguiling bathroom. The bunch of garden roses in their blue and white goblet and the blue-lined mug are the only deviations from the green and white theme, for even the towel is more of a 'greenery-yallery' colour and blends with the paler green of the cabinet above. The general effect of the delicate build-up of shades and gentle contrasts is quiet yet refreshing, like a peaceful, leafy garden – the very model of a country bathroom.

ABOVE A simple modern version of the
'greenery-yallery' theme: softly green-
veined yellow walls, green leaves, green
and white throw, yellow pottery, nice
natural cane and matting and pale
stripped pine.

LEFT Another fresh build-up of greens, this
time in the peppermint class: gentle,
harmonious shades of green in mini-
patterns are used for the soft furnishings.
The same main shade of green is used in
the wallpaper, but this time it is mixed
with a levelling umber and accented by
the mirror frame. The fresh green of the
fern and foliage is echoed in the stripes of
the rug, and against all this verdure the
pinky-apricot alternative stripes, the
natural colours of matting and baskets
become like glimpses of bare earth seen
through a frame of leaves.

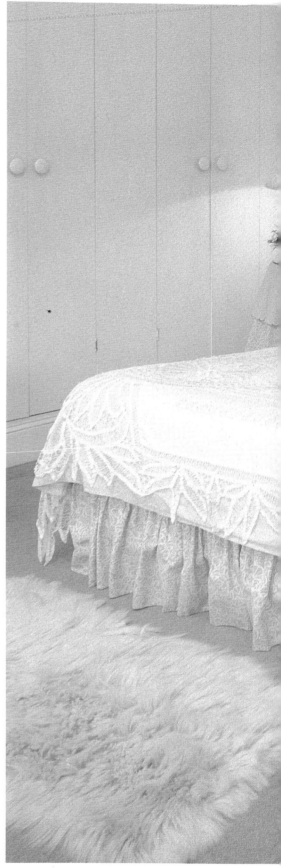

ABOVE Green-ferned fabric mixed with a healthy collection of the real thing is a happy conceit in this sparkling corner. Note how the fern overskirt is offset by a multi-flowered cotton in blue, pink and yellow as well as green which is echoed by the vase of flowers above. The general effect, together with the coia matting and natural wicker chairs, makes for another serendipitous composition of fresh green shades and quiet contrasts. Natural woody shades work well with almost any green and here give the impression of a bright garden corner, sheltered by trees.

RIGHT Pale, pale green and creamy apple white make good companions for bedrooms, being naturally fresh and pristine, not to mention proverbially restful. The simplicity of this scheme is underscored by the repetition of the same soft green for bedhead, valance (bed ruffle) and the skirts of the bedside table, contrasted with the darker olive of chair and picture frame and the greeny white of the walls. The creamy fur of the goatskin rug provides a touch of textured warmth to offset the cool effect created by so much green and white.

ACCENT

Green is the great freshener. A bunch of greenery in a roomful of dark colours, for example umber walls, reddish rugs and those rosy country house chintzes, breathes life and vigour into the entire scheme. Or add fresh green to soft greys and blues, a dash of green to aquamarine, a large leafy plant to apricot walls. Touches of green have an instantly cooling effect upon red.

In a creamy neutral space a touch of green brings to light fine nuances which would otherwise have remained unnoticed. The slimmest green binding livens up chintz curtains; crisp green industrial rubber flooring gives a vivid contrast to an otherwise stark black and white hi-tech room.

Just think of any flower, plant, fruit or tree; or the gamut of colours – purples and pinks, reds and yellows, oranges and blues – in a herbaceous border with its framework of green; or the last vestiges of green in an autumn flurry of tawny yellows, browns and crimson madders; or spring green against the greyish brown of trunks and branches; May leaves against the pale red-streaked rose of apple blossom, and summer leaves against strawberries, raspberries, peaches, apricots and cherries, whether their colours are dark red and mouth-staining or fresh yellow and red. Translate any of these images into furnishings and you will be producing charming rooms for years to come.

Green with white, of course, is one of the most beloved schemes of all. An otherwise all-white kitchen, with green plastic handles on the cupboards and green taps (faucets) looks forever neat and fresh. A white bathroom with green towels, green and white tiles or white tiles with a green border will have much the same effect.

An all-white living room with green cushions or woodwork and a mass of green leaves and plants looks perennially cool in a hot climate or by a beach. Or you can ring the changes with a green and white cotton fabric juxtaposed with plain white and plain green, with a softening touch provided by the neutral tones of coia matting and cane.

In a warm peach, apricot or soft pink bedroom, a few touches of bright green, perhaps in the fabrics used, will freshen the colours instantly and bring them to life in the same way as a few leaves give fruit in a bowl the air of having been plucked only minutes ago.

LEFT There can hardly be a fresher accent than green plants in a mostly white room. The plants here link pleasantly and immediately with the greenery outside, as well as softening the impact of the black lines of the chair and the dark mass of the painting. Restraint is the key to success in this stylish room.

ABOVE The bright emerald stripes of the green and white tablecloth in this mainly natural wood kitchen add a lively touch of colour as well as blending with the leafy exterior. This accent of green is repeated by the odd plant cascading from a shelf, green pottery and storage jars, and by the khaki green of the lamp shade and refrigerator. The composition of natural wood, white walls and pale quarry tiles is very pleasant, and the touches of green add to the restfulness in what is generally one of the busiest rooms of the house.

EQUAL TONES

We know that green is a receding colour and it is commonly thought of as a cool one, so it is logical to use it in conjunction with blue, another cool and receding colour, quite apart from the fact that the juxtaposition of greens and blues is one of the most natural combinations in the world around us.

The immediate thought is the clear blue of the summer sky with the strong green of midsummer leaves and grass, but there are also the purply blue and green of heather and Scottish hills, the hazy blue greens of the Italian lakes, the piercing blue of gentians in Swiss meadows, the extraordinary clarity of dark green cypresses and dark blue sparkling sea which can be seen in so many Mediterranean resorts.

Any of these combinations, translated into soft furnishings and wall colourings, make memorable schemes. They are especially suitable for summer rooms and hot climates, but they need not be relegated to eternal summer: the addition of good lighting, firelight, the sparkle of a mirror and perhaps the flash of red flowers makes them welcoming all year round.

Green and yellow is another obvious combination to use in a harmonious scheme, since yellow is green's other neighbour in the colour spectrum. Green, yellow and white, or green, blue and yellow look fresh and lively.

Other tones in the same colour range which look both fresh and warm in combination, and are therefore ideal for darker rooms, are greens, yellows and lilacs, or green, apricot and blue.

The autumnal palette is a constant source of inspiration: the deep rose and madder of the Virginia creeper, the russet glory of a wood in October with its tangle of green, yellow, Indian red and tawny brown. No single colour overrides any other, but the green acts as an anchor, a calming influence on the riot of autumnal splendour. Use the reds and yellows against dark green walls, for example, or a deep green carpet or painted floor.

Soft pale greens also look charming with greys and rose, as in a gentle sunset over a darkening landscape. Or there is the soft green of lichen against grey rocks; moss on grey stone walls; ivy rambling over mellow brick, or green trees against grey pavements.

LEFT The bright green, yellow and red in this wallpaper are matched by the equally strong plain colours of the window frame, sofa and vases. The cheerfully informal decoration would look charming in a country cottage or in a child's bedroom.

RIGHT If the room to the left is a conscious interplay of colour repeating colour, the room to the right is an equally carefully thought-out composition of both shapes and colours, although in this instance the general harmony is broken here and there by definite punctuations, as in the black cat in the centre above the black fireplace surround and the black cats at top left and bottom right of the picture grouping. Then, too, the group of pictures is itself framed in a way by the pineapple stencilled border all around the top of the wall, with its punctilious composition of green, blue and apricot, bordered by the apricot picture rail which is, in turn, matched by the skirting boards (base boards) below and, of course, the tiles. The effect is disarmingly casual, but the effort must have been created with every attention to detail.

ABOVE The soft golden tone of the natural wood and the floor tiles, teamed up with the soft green of the walls, produces an atmosphere of calm tranquility in this quietly elegant hall.

RIGHT Soft jade green and apricot with occasional dashes of creamy honeysuckle yellow blend very happily together in this bedroom corner. The painted chest of drawers faithfully reflects the background green of the fabric, and the interesting medley of related colours on top of the chest is again repeated in the painting above and in the fabric flowers clustered in the old box.

ABOVE Soft apricot, terracotta and muted green set the scene in this marvellously co-ordinated room. The green on the wall – which is in fact a mural – is echoed by the green of the lampshade, the green stripe in the upholstery fabric, the French windows and the interesting honeycombe pattern of the window frame. Again, the expanse of apricot and the terracotta detail in the mural are repeated in the sofa and chair cushions. The softness of the colours, reminiscent of a townscape or village in the fading sunlight of the evening, contributes greatly to the comfortable and relaxing atmosphere of this well-designed room.

BLUE

COOL, SOPHISTICATED, HEAVENLY,
ELEGANT, CLASSY, FORMAL

The word blue instantly conjures up images of skies: the pale blue-grey dawn, the azure of a clear summer's day, the grapey blue of impending storms, the deep velvety damson blue of a warm night. But blue is also the colour of sun-dazzled water with its affinity to precious stones: the limpid translucency of aquamarine, the dark profundity of sapphire, the brilliant clarity of turquoise and the swirled surface of lapis lazuli.

Blue flowers abound, and many of them have lent their name to a particular shade of blue, like hyacinth blue, which was much favoured for paint and fabrics during the British Regency and French Empire period, or orchid, a light lavender which was the chic colour of the 1920s.

To Kandinsky, co-founder of the Blau Reiter group of revolutionary artists in Germany in 1911, blue was heavenly, pure and infinite, suggestive of eternal peace; but like so many colours, blue has contradictory connotations. It has an intellectual (bluestocking) and aristocratic (blue blood) aura; on the other hand, it is also associated with depression (feeling blue) and indecency (blue movies). In spite of its psychological anomalies, however, blue always has been, and remains, a classy colour.

The Chinese obtained the Nankin blue for their blue and white porcelain from a salt of

cobalt, and this was the first Chinese colour to be successfully copied by the European potteries.

The Persians, of course, favoured a piercing turquoise blue as a background for their ceramics and tiles for centuries, the colour being copied in France in the eighteenth century at the royal porcelain factory of Sèvres.

Sèvres was also famous for the deep, rich royal blue background and for bleu celeste a cerulean (sky) blue first developed in 1772. Sky blue was enormously popular for wall colouring and for fabrics in eighteenth-century France. Another favourite was peacock blue, which was first imported into Venice from China in the form of greenish-blue iridescent silks. From Venice it filtered into France, where it was much in vogue in the late seventeenth and early eighteenth centuries.

Mauve was discovered quite by chance in 1856 when William Henry Perkins, a scientist, was trying to produce artificial quinine. The delicate purple-violet hue became all the rage in decorating, resulting in the famous turn-of-the-century 'mauve' generation.

Blue is a primary colour and its complement is orange, a combination of the other two primaries, red and yellow. Blue is a receding colour and appears to push walls back, giving an impression of space and coolness.

SHADES AND CONTRASTS

Sky, from the pallor of dawn to the depth of midnight, is blue. Forget-me-nots, violets, delphiniums and harebells all fall under the same blue aegis, as do aquamarines, amethysts and sapphires. The shades of blue cover an enormous range, and as they range so they can be contrasted with each other and with a great many other colours to interesting and varied effect. In this striking fabric they are richly put together with plummy reds and orange reds, golds and greys. Here, plain blue is used to anchor a vibrant scheme, in which the blue is emphatically and unequivocally that of a hot Indian summer.

ACCENT

Blue and white, blue on white and blue with white are
perennial favourites for room schemes: soft but lively;
gentle and fresh; cool, demure and inviting. Blue
accents in a white room can hardly go wrong.
Whatever the blues and whatever the whites, it is a
combination of two stylish colours which tend to
make rooms appear larger and more spacious. A touch
of blue can be used to anchor a white scheme,
preventing the white from becoming too dazzling but
preserving the airiness and lightness of the overall
impression, but blue is also a good accent with
yellow, cream or red.

EQUAL TONES

Blue and rose work felicitously together as equal
tones, as can blue and yellow. In this fabric, all three
hold equal weight, and the result is lively without
being brash: the greyish tint in the blue softens it,
making it a natural companion to the muted, gentle
pink, while the yellow lightens the other colours and
blends with them, like sunlight on a garden in early
summer. The result is a scheme which is both lively
and gentle and in which the recessive characteristics of
the blue are nicely balanced by the advancing pink
and yellow, which also prevent the blue from
appearing in any way cold.

SHADES AND CONTRASTS

Blue and white is the immediately obvious choice for any contrasting blue scheme, whether it is the sunny look engendered by clear sky blue with sparkling white, or the crisper, clean-cut navy.

Blue and white china and pottery has always been popular as an inspiration, but ideas for room schemes can equally well be gleaned from the brilliant turquoise and aubergines of the Chinese Kang H'si period, at the turn of the seventeenth century; the dark blues, apricots and gold of Japanese Imari porcelain of the early eighteenth century, or the magnificent blue and orange tiles of the Moorish palace of the Alhambra in Granada.

Alternatively, a trip to any oriental carpet store should provide a plethora of schemes: the powder blue, contrasting pinky beiges, dark blue and Indian reds of Kashan and Hamadan rugs; the beautiful creams and turquoises peculiar to the silk rugs of the city of Qum, or Turkey rugs in dark blues and reds. The latter might inspire dark blue walls; red, blue and grey fabrics mixed with blue and white plates, enlivened by yellow flowers and glossy green leaves.

As always, nature is an inspired provider of ideas for schemes centering on blue. The obvious one, of course, is the sky arching serenely over trees and fields. Plain blue walls and ceiling, or a marbled or paint-effect paper with a white trim, and a green carpet used in conjunction with soft furnishings in varying shades of blue would be pleasantly calm and peaceful. Add further contrasts, using red flowers, large plants or paintings which are predominantly red to add a touch of warmth.

Another obvious theme are the aquamarines, sands and rosy ochres of the sea shore. These could be expressed by sand-coloured walls and woodwork, with a pale blue carpet or rug, pale aquamarine or sky blue armchairs and a slightly darker blue sofa. Contrast these main colours with pale terracotta or peach cushions and masses of creamy yellow roses, tinged with red.

Gentle yet luxurious schemes can be inspired by blueberries and cream or the pinky blue of thick cream squashed into blackberries, translated into inky blues, rose and cream fabric, stormy blue walls, and indigo carpet and the contrast of bright blue and green leaves.

LEFT Blue and white china, blue and terracotta, blue and rose, blue and apricot, whatever shape and size it is, blue and white porcelain and its variations have always been a source of easy inspiration for room schemes, or, if not for whole schemes, for contrast. Here, the stripped wood shelves are filled with a pleasing collection of china in varying shades of blue along with a posy of violets and an opalescent blue-green vase. The touches of gold and apricot, in the china and in the lamp, provide a pleasing contrast to this attractive mixture of blues.

RIGHT Another vivid colourway in the coordinating collection also seen on page 24, this is a very far cry from the traditional blue with white. Here is a room which successfully repudiates any notion of blue as a cool colour. In this company it positively zings and is used, like a black, to bring out the warmth of the reds, pinks and tans. The interesting fact is that the floral design of the throw, in spite of its geometric background, does not look so far removed from the pot of anemones and zinnias on the table, and although the initial impact of the entire scene is about as far removed from nature as a Picasso portrait, it ultimately has the same effect as a large bunch of brightly coloured flowers.

ABOVE More cool blues: this time the soft blue of the mottled bathroom tiles frames the green view outside and contrasts gently with the natural stone surrounding the windows. The addition of lavender in the glass of the central jar and in the soaps to the right gently sharpens the image. The result is cool yet inviting, the ideal scheme for a bathroom in hot sunny climate.

LEFT On another altogether cooler note than the previous page these pale pastel fabrics and rug mix blues, greens and lavenders as hazily as a field of gentians emerging from the last wisps of summer mist. But the general effect is restful rather than cold, soft and comfortable and generally relaxing. Note how the clear green of the ferns and the purples and violets of the flowers stand out against the softness of the whole.

ABOVE The general blue and white theme of this kitchen is warmed by the pale terracotta floor, the butcher block work surface and the baskets, and is given a sharp focus with the black lacquered bentwood chairs and the collection of black pottery. The soft, cool recessive blue, however, effectively prevents the rows of cupboards from overwhelming the entire scene, but makes this kitchen look spacious and welcoming; a place where the family could gather comfortably.

ACCENT

Blue is a subtle accent colour in many decorative schemes, adding depth, calm and quiet or a flash of gaiety, according to the shade. Although it is as natural a companion to white as cream to coffee, it can equally well accent an otherwise yellow and pink room, or give apricot an anchoring quiet.

A vivid hyacinth or delphinium blue gives definition and panache to aubergine walls, just as pale blue livens up navy or purply grape. Add a few blue and white plates to any rosy chintz room and you will immediately have given it more interest. Back this up with a pot full of blue hydrangeas and the scheme is somehow much more complex. A bowlful of hyacinths, cornflowers or delphiniums looks as marvellous against lemon yellow walls as blue feathers against yellow in a canary or parrot.

A bunch of irises, pansies or some other purplish flower looks stunning in a mainly honeysuckle and peach room. Clear sky blue, of course, brings any terracotta scheme to life, being redolent of warm southern colours: burnt red tiles against azure skies. Conversely, Matisse sometimes used dark Prussian blue to warm up his entire palette of colours through contrast.

Clear blue, perhaps in cushions, cheers up a nutmeg sofa or chair, and any one of the gamut of blues from palest grey blue through lavender to purple adds softness and interest to greys and camels. At the lighter end of the neutral scale, a mainly cream room with flashes of turquoise always looks bright and airy and well cared for.

Cornflower blue looks good against wicker, rush, cane and old pine, as do cornflowers straggling through fields of wheat. And if you look at violets and snowdrops pushing up through wet spring grass you are already provided with a sweet fresh scheme, just as you might be inspired by the wild intense lavender that grows through hedgerows alongside fields of sun-bleached maize under a burnished, cloudless sky.

Perhaps one of the nicest thoughts about blue as an accent colour was summarized by Van Gogh in one of his letters about his house in Arles: 'Inside it's completely whitewashed and the floor is red brick. *And the intense blue sky above.*' One has an instant picture of Mediterranean sky framed by windows.

LEFT This play on blues, clear-cut variations on a theme, looks both graphic and charming set against the plain white background, and it is all the better for being framed by the pale pine of the cabinet and punctuated by the green of the leaves. There is no doubt that blue, any blue, is an exceptional accent colour against any white or cream.

RIGHT The pair of blue coffee tables provides the focal point in this sitting room, which is predominantly furnished in greens and neutrals. The colours of the walls, curtains, carpet and upholstery are so soft that without the hard-edged contrast of the blue the room would have looked too bland.

ABOVE The very graphic quality of blue accents against white are again demonstrated in this cool yet charming dining room/kitchen. But note how the sharp clear blue of the china and napkins looks quite warm against the grey blues of the cushions on the cane chairs. This is a cheerfully informal setting, a relaxing place to start and end the day, equally comfortable in winter and summer.

RIGHT This is another demonstration of the versatility of blue and its wide range, for the deep heathery blue in sofa, rug and paintings again looks positively warm against the creamy walls and polished bare wood floor of this room, with its natural matchstick blinds, stripped pine and terracotta pots. The distinct rose tint in the blue is, of course, nursed along by the additional rose in rug, cushions (pillows) and flowers, but that only goes to show what a chameleon colour blue can be. The same shades used with greens and whites could look as cool as the slope of a Scottish mountain.

EQUAL TONES

The Impressionists, who were obsessed with colour, believed that juxtaposed complementary colours intensify each other when used in large enough areas, whereas they fuse into a neutral tone when used in smaller quantities. They tended to ban neutral hues from their palettes, tingeing their shadows with colours complementary to the object casting the shadow. Manet's stunning 'River at Argenteuil', painted in 1874, was therefore executed entirely in primary colours and mixtures of these colours, so that the blue and mauve brushstrokes of the water contrast with the yellow and orange strokes of the boats and masts and their shadows.

This kind of theorizing has a lot to teach us about using similarly equal tones in the right proportions in room decoration. Lovely domestic juxtapositions can be created by carefully studying such paintings and noting the actual visual effects produced by the colours rather than the effects which you would expect them to produce.

Another helpful way to study the interaction of colours, especially of blue mixed with other colours, is to observe a landscape or town scene in the gentle dying light of early evening. The sun-bleached houses of southern Europe clustering on their reddish cliffs are tinged with a blue shadow in the fading light. Trees, too, have a bluish cast. The same colouring – terracottas, blues, bluey greens – applied to a room, gives it a warm roseate look, an air of time-lessness and calm.

The countries of the south are also superb sources of inspiration for schemes using vivid colours, mostly because the bright sun and deep blue sky call out for bright strong colours to match their intensity. People living in constantly sunny climates tend to have a much surer and bolder touch with bright colours than people living in temperate climates. Anyone interested in blue schemes, or schemes in which blue at least plays an important role, would be well advised to study paintings, fabrics and landscapes of the sun: the flamboyant dresses of Spanish ladies, etched against a bright blue sky; the vivid blue and yellow of Hispanic tiles, splashed with water from fountains so that they gleam and dance in the sun, or the rich colours of the miniatures painted for the Mughal rulers of India.

ABOVE **If blue is a favourite accent colour, it is just as good set on equal terms with other colours, when it acts as an excellent balancer. Blue-green Roman blinds (shades) in this bay window make a good foil for the kaleidoscope of soft cushions (pillows) tossed onto the charcoal grey window seat.**

RIGHT **You virtually live inside your own art in this Bloomsbury-like breakfast room where walls and fabric are both covered in free-style painting (the curtains are homespun cotton which have been dyed and painted with a fabric paint, as is the cushion on the chair), and even the furniture is an illusion in the sense that the table and table lamp were actually made from plywood and broomsticks painted with black eggshell and varnished with a satin finish. But apart from the virtuosity of it all, note how the blues give a cool stability to the other colours.**

ABOVE **Blue** grey, charcoal and beige are soberly mixed in a diagonally striped design and make a fitting background for the angular glass table and charcoal-coloured chairs in a generally grey-blue room. Note how the muted colouring softens and muffles the hard angles of the furnishings.

ABOVE Blue and rose cotton covers for two mattresses make a striking splash of colour as well, one presumes, as an effective bed in an otherwise all-white studio space. Rose, grey and white pillows and a blue lampshade add to the liveliness of the scene, as do items in the shelving and the rack of clothes.

LEFT Pinks and blues are the predominant colours in this comfortable room, where everything is beautifully co-ordinated. The blue curtains tone with the carpets and are echoed by the two cushions (pillows) in the sofa. They also match the blue pattern on the printed wallpaper, the blue stripe in the upholstery fabric and the piping. The pink stripe in the upholstery fabric is repeated in the curtain binding and tie-backs and, as a finishing touch, in the teacups. To complete the picture, a beautiful patchwork wallhanging combines the colours of the room and gives emphasis to the pink and blue.

RED

WARM, BOLD, SUMPTUOUS, VIBRANT,
FESTIVE, PASSIONATE

*Red starts with the delicate pink of wild roses,
meanders through the velvety hybrids, rosy red
bricks, poppies, red peppers, corals, luscious
cherries, strawberries, raspberries, autumn hips,
Bordeaux, Burgundies and other red wines,
deepens to the garnet and ruby of jewels, and
tails off to the reddish-purple of aubergines
(eggplant), the bloomy skins of plums and the
sheen of dark grapes and amethysts.*

*It is a colour of strong contrasts – a dashing,
military colour at one end of the scale, and at
the other end pink, a hue which is traditionally
connected with softness and femininity.*

*Red is emboldening, stirring: the red badge of
courage, the dashing Scarlet Pimpernel, the flag
of martyrs and of revolutionaries, the colour of
danger and of sin.*

*The Romans loved red and used a variety of
shades, including the rich, glowing Pompeiian
red, the deep red purple of Tyrian red, which
was the symbol of the Caesars and of rulers ever
since, the fuchsia pink which was the 'purple' of
lesser mortals, the red porphyry which was
introduced from Egypt by the Emperor Claudius
and, of course, terracotta, which ranges from
pale reddish buff to deep brownish red and
which remains of all colours the one most
redolent of Mediterranean countries.*

The Chinese produced a rich mottled blood-

red glaze called sang de boeuf, or ox blood, which turned into sherry brown in areas of coagulation. It originated in the K'ang Hsi era, at the turn of the seventeenth century and became especially popular in the nineteenth century and again in the 1930s.

Chinese red, however, is the brilliant orange red of oriental lacquer, much favoured since the eighteenth-century vogue for chinoiserie and fashionable in Regency England, when whole rooms were painted and glazed in the colour.

Oriental artists and craftsmen have never had any inhibitions about mixing red and pink, whether in Persian or Turkish carpets, Chinese embroideries or nineteenth-century Japanese colour prints. In the West, however, it is a much rarer combination, though it was used to stunning effect in the 1950s and 1960s by David Hicks, whose mixtures of dark and light reds with fuchsia pinks, and of aubergine (eggplant), red and orange dazzled the post-war generation, just as Elsa Schiaparelli's shocking pink had stunned the fashionable world of the 1930s.

Red is a primary, its complementary colour being green, a mixture of blue and yellow. It is an advancing colour and so warm that experiments have shown that people in a red room feel warmer than people in a blue room kept at the same temperature.

SHADES AND CONTRASTS

The varied colours within the red range, from pink to deep plum and from scarlet to the orange red of nasturtiums, blend and contrast interestingly with each other, although the drama can sometimes be carried too far for harmony. In this instance, striking slashes of red are contrasted with deep grey and orange yellow on white, and set against a fine red striped paper. The white helps to make the red and orange even more vivid and glowing, while the grey prevents the combination from appearing glaringly bright. The overall effect is certainly good and lively and would be best used in a darkish space.

ACCENT

It is hardly necessary to repeat that red warms and livens. Red accents, such as flowers, cushions, trims and door handles or touches of red in a fabric, will liven up paler colours in an instant. Flowers are a particularly good way of adding a touch of red to a predominantly green room: the leaves blend in with the surroundings and provide an entirely natural link between the décor and the splash of red, whether this is the vivid red of carnations and tulips or the softer, pinky reds of roses. In a similar way, a pale blue room, while the perfect antidote to an overhot summer, may need touches of red in winter.

EQUAL TONES

Red often works more harmoniously on equal terms with other colours in its rose guise. Just as garden pinks have grey-green leaves and stems and the underside of rose leaves are a softer, paler green than the surface, so the different shades of rose and pink work well with soft greens as in this fabric. The gentle pastels of this design, with its simple, stylized flowers reminiscent of a patchwork quilt, and the fresh pink and white wallpaper would look pleasant and relaxing in a bedroom. The whole effect is warm, but the green and white balance the pink and prevent it from becoming too cloying.

SHADES AND CONTRASTS

According to Chevreul's theories in his great nineteenth-century treatise on colour, if a dot of a colour, for instance green, is placed next to a large area of its complementary colour, in this case red, the colour of the larger area becomes more vibrant. However, if small amounts of complementary colours are used next to each other they fuse and become a tertiary colour, more of an impression, and it is certainly true that a basically red room is toned down and made altogether more restful when mixed with a good deal of green and blue. Equally, it becomes more brilliant when given just a small contrast of green, perhaps in the form of a plant.

Natural inspiration for schemes using reds and pinks can be found in numerous trees and plants. There are peonies with their pink, cherry or crimson flowers, or cyclamen, with rich pink or carmine flowers and variegated leaves. The latter suggests a scheme using a mixture of dark and light greens together with a bright pink or red. Other designs could be developed from the image of soft fruit orchards laden with cherries, damsons or Victoria plums fringed by thick green leaves growing from grey-green branches.

Then there is the vast range of ornamental cherries and plums, which display stunning contrasts between the pale pink or rose of the thickly clustered flowers, the bronze green of the leaves and the darker reddish brown of the bark, outlined against a clear blue sky. This would make a pleasant colour combination for a bedroom, with walls of soft plain pink or a rag-rubbed effect, fabrics in blue, green and pink for the curtains and bedspread, red mahogany furniture and a bronzy-green carpet.

Inspiration also comes from the earth itself, from the red clay of Italy, Greece and Egypt, burnt by sun from a hot blue sky; from Petra, that 'rose red city half as old as time', the red sandstone of which is coloured in swirls of blackberry, deep pink, damask and ochre, or from the pink and grey-white marble of Verona.

Above all, red is identified with roses: old rose gardens or crimson roses rambling up through an apple tree, inspiring the ever popular English chintzes.

LEFT A plethora of pinky-rose fabrics, quite apart from the roses themselves, gives this corner a, yes, roseate glow with or without the romantic lamplight. The grey of the lamp base and the natural cane make a good contrast to the build-up of sunset shades.

RIGHT Pale rose walls, co-ordinating rose and green cottons with an unusual earthenware plant container and a much deeper rose and green carpet contribute towards a room that looks good in all seasons, all weathers. The rose and green paper border placed half way up the walls balances the same border used as a dado rail lower down and helps to minimize the effect of a particularly lofty ceiling, as, of course, do the colours, for any rose gives an instant impression of warmth and easiness to a room.

LEFT Walls painted the colour of terracotta flower pots in a spacious hall are cooled by the natural coia matting on the floor and contrast well with the handsome mahogany bookshelves, the gilded nineteenth-century chairs and the old blue and white Delft tiles in the fireplace. The strong lines of the black marble fireplace are balanced by the Helene Feisenmeier painting above, and note how the lowered end of the hallway, down a shallow flight of stairs, is delineated by aubergine (eggplant) paint on the walls and pine instead of the darker shade of mahogany.

RIGHT The reddish-orange shade used for the walls of this sitting room is contrasted with the basically grey-green cotton of the curtains, the wing chair and the strong blue background of the chair in the foreground. The careful build-up of warm shades and cooler contrasts makes an essentially warm room which could be cooled down in high summer with the addition of more plants, and, for example, a pile of cooler-coloured cushions (pillows) on the long sofa and a rug with an off-white or string background, for example an Indian dhurrie.

ACCENT

A touch of red instantly adds life, not to say festivity, to a scheme. Red flowers or cushions, red mounted prints or a painting which is primarily red immediately make a room which is basically brown warmer and more embracing.

This effect applies to virtually any red added to any brown, ranging from beige or pale coffee to dark umber. Add touches of lacquer red to grey or to grey and black and you achieve a definite oriental distinction. Add terracotta to blue and yellow and you have instantly created an air of Mediterranean charm.

Red accents in an all-white room like a kitchen or bathroom are innately cheerful. Lay a browny-red tiled floor in a predominantly natural wood and white kitchen, add a few red enamelled cook pots, and the room leaps to life. Hang red towels in a white bathroom, add a red-bordered white blind, and it will look fresh and cheerful. If you put a touch of green in the white paint, the red accents will really glow.

Dark blue walls with a red and blue Turkey carpet look suitably bookish in a study or library, just as a rose pink, red and aubergine (eggplant) rag rug gives instant pep to aubergine walls. And a red and green patterned carpet provides a vigorous counterpoint in a room with dark green walls.

In the eighteenth century, Robert Adam frequently added small areas of soft pink to his mainly pale green and white designs and touches of pink certainly help to take the edge off the coolness of pastel greens and blues.

In a primarily aquamarine room, jugs of red flowers or branches of berries will create a warm sparkly atmosphere in winter, but just one red book left on a table in a room of almost any colour you care to mention will work like an exclamation point in the same manner as a red carnation in the buttonhole on a dark suit. Van Gogh, that master of colour, understood this so well. His signature in red on a blue seascape and the thin red rim round a rowing boat added life to the entire picture.

In just the same way, a touch of red added to the design in fabrics or wallpapers will give the print extra clarity and warmth, an important point to remember when you want to use warm but light colours in a north-facing or otherwise dark room.

ABOVE Schiaparelli's shocking pink has the same enlivening effect in this very graphic room of dark greys and moles. Note the interesting juxtaposition of the aubergine (eggplant) vases filled with purple flowers. These, combined with the brilliant pink, give the greys a purplish cast of their own, whereas an equally brilliant yellow, for example, would have made the greys look both blacker and more crisp.

LEFT Brilliant red tulips, bright pink cushions (pillows) and red stripes in the sofa fabric, as well as red and white china in the pine cabinet, add sharpening accents to the otherwise golden tones of this living room, enhanced by the natural sunlight filtering through the window. The red and pink act as instant liveners. The result is a successful blend of traditional and modern design.

ABOVE Red, apricot and yellow flowers are specially chosen to accent and underline the colours of the chintz at the windows in this corner.

LEFT The rose accents of the patchwork quilt, scatter cushions (pillows) and flowers are particularly pretty in this creamy bedroom, with its long airy windows and bare polished floor boards. The open cane bedhead and chair consolidate the overall feeling of cheerful lightness and, although the room is sparsley furnished, it looks welcoming.

RIGHT The total look here is uncompromisingly modern – only a few very subtle, geometric patterns have been used together with plains to produce a hi-tech effect. The room is predominantly black and white, with a natural wood floor that softens the stark appearance. The splashes of bright red in roller blind, book shelves, picture and rug add life to the scheme.

ABOVE The red and blue designs of the quilt and the tablecloth, and the rosy red of the dried flowers and herbs in the bouquet by the bed, add a subtle but lively accent to the sumptuous creaminess of this bedroom, providing an essential touch of warmth and interest to what could otherwise be too bland and lifeless. The cream, in turn, softens the brightness of the red.

LEFT Red on white always looks fresh and cheerful in a kitchen, and the red accents here are no exception. The cherry trim around the cabinets and the matching handles look handsome in conjunction with the red and white floor and the deep rose tiles between work top and units. The large fern behind the lattice divider adds the requisite touch of green.

EQUAL TONES

Red has such a forceful image that it is hard to imagine it being on an equal footing with any other colour, yet in fact it works outstandingly well with its fellow primaries. This is graphically exemplified in Piet Mondrian's 'Composition with Red, Yellow and Blue', painted in 1921, which consists of black and white rectangles with one blue square, two red rectangles adjoining each other, and one yellow rectangle.

Different reds mix extraordinarily well: burgundy red and crimson, ox blood and pink, Chinese lacquer red and very dark red, orange and red. But it is pinks which are most often used with soft shades of other colours, such as grey, powder blue, mauve or green.

The warm rose pink called Rose Pompadour, created at the Sèvres porcelain factory and named after its patroness, Madame de Pompadour, is often mixed with just such colours in a deliberately feminine room. Try a rose pink pattern on walls and bedspread, a blue and white carpet, rose and white blinds or curtains, and cushions in lavender blue or deep rose.

Green is the natural complement of red, and any red looks good with any green. The image of rosy apples weighing down the trees in an orchard can be recreated in a room with lacquered green walls and red and green upholstery.

Red and blue in any shade or combination seems to work almost as well as red and green. The brick red paint so often found on the barns and clapboard houses of rural America is often used in conjunction with a stormy blue which is also characteristic of New England. Note how pink edges into blues in hydrangea flowers; how poppies look in a hedge alongside the wild bright blue of cornflowers; the mixture of salmony red, blue and gold on Japanese Imari porcelain, and the merging of reds and blues in heather-covered Scottish hills.

Bright red and yellow appear hard-edged, clean-cut and aggressive, but there is also the gentleness of the yellow merging into pink of a papaya, or pink and yellow roses. These combinations look particularly pretty, warm and fresh in interiors, translated into bedroom or living room walls, rugs and florals.

LEFT Pink and yellow with a vivid splash of brilliant grass green look suitably cheerful and lively in this small child's room. Note the exactly right touch of coolness with the slim trim of pale pistachio green all around the edge of the chest of drawers, and the areas of yellow, which add variety without detracting from the warmth of the prevailing rose pink.

RIGHT Baskets of purplish dried herbs and flowers slung from purple-painted trellis are interestingly juxtaposed with large rose cushions and a comfortable pile of rose and blue cushions (pillows) in this luxuriant conservatory/garden room. The odd touch of sapphire blue in the stripped pine floor seems to throw the rest of the softer colours into a gentle and harmonious relief, as do the terracotta urns and the sharp fresh green leaves of the plants.

ABOVE Pink gladioli and eucalyptus in a
skinny glass vase seem to light up the
large expanse of creamy yellow. Together
with the dark, rich pink cushion (pillow),
they are strongly reminiscent of the roses
to be found in an old-fashioned shrub-rose
garden, creating an atmosphere which is
essentially warm and relaxing.

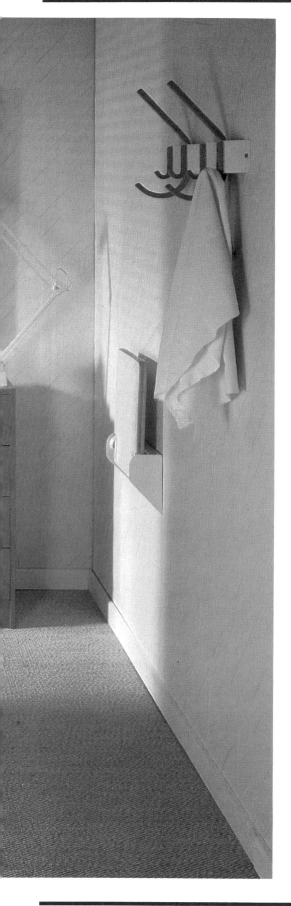

LEFT The muted fuchsia-painted chest at the end of this narrow room surmounted by the subtler colours of the painting gives distinction to an otherwise anonymous little space. Note how the upholstery on the chair combines the colours of both, as do the colours in the subtle pattern on the wallpaper. This is an excellent example of how a narrow space can be made to look larger by using very light wall colours.

ABOVE Rose-painted walls and the yellow of the lampshade, pure papaya colours, set the scene in this warm bedroom, where they blend into the paler pink chintz of the bedside tablecloth and the pale bed linen and paintings. The effect is certainly cheerful.

NEUTRALS

CALM, RESTFUL, NATURAL,
COMFORTABLE, ELEGANT

*Neutrals are the anchoring colours of nature:
the soft browns and duns of earth; the bleached
beiges of rocks, stones and pebbles; the yellowed
white of sand and dust; the golden hues of
polished wood, and the warm tones of clay.*

*The range really extends from white through
to black, with the gamut of greys, creams,
mushroom, camel, tans and nutmeg to dark
umbers in between. For the purposes of
decoration, however, it makes sense to hive off
the more dramatic extremes of black and white,
and their mixture grey, into a separate chapter,
covering only the softer, brownish neutrals here.*

*Although these gentle hues are restful and
earthy, they are also the colours of many living
things, from the speckled feathers of thrushes
and starlings or the subtle shades on a moth's
wings to the gleaming, sensuous browns of sleek
furs, the lively tans and chestnuts of handsome
horses and the shiny richness of conkers.*

*In the hands of the practised, neutrals can be
instruments of true elegance and take on a life
of their own. They can either tone down
brighter colours or bring them into focus, and
on the positive side their muted hues are the
perfect means of exposing form, contour and
texture. It is not just the absence of leaves but
also the predominance of neutrals which throws
a winter landscape into sharp relief, revealing*

the contours of hills and ploughed fields.

The Japanese are masters of the art of using neutrals. The most famous example is perhaps the temple garden at Ryoanji, a space about the size of a tennis court, covered with a bed of pebbles raked in a uniform direction. There are no plants or trees, just 15 stones in small groups, but the garden designer Russell Page calls it 'an expression of faith and space and time and yet garden in its very essence'.

In the West neutrals were for centuries the hallmark of the poor, while the rich favoured expensive dyes and imported silks and papers for furnishing. In the 1920s, however, under the influence of the Bauhaus school of art and architecture in Germany, neutrals like cream, stone, ecru and biscuit became the height of fashion. This theme was continued in the International Style of the 1950s and 1960s, when almost the only colour allowed was the green provided by plants, the rich brown leather of the tubular metal chairs or the brown and white calfskin on the Corbusier chairs.

The tones may be muted, yet a roomful of neutrals can be lively yet relaxing. It is worth noting that many great artists, including Leonardo da Vinci and El Greco, achieved their effects with a palette composed largely of these subtle shades.

SHADES AND CONTRASTS

The word neutral sounds so nebulous that it is often hard to remember how richly varied neutrals can in fact be in terms of decoration. The gamut runs from pale creams to deep umbers, with nutmeg, ginger and chestnut in between. Or think of the difference between pearl and dark grey, camel and cane. Camel wallpaper here contrasts gently with the cane chair, and the tans and chestnuts of the fabric are given a kind of three-dimensional depth by the contrasting blues and greens. The result is a rich, mellow, yet restful combination of autumn colours which would warm up a cool room without overwhelming it.

ACCENT

Although accents are usually stronger and more vibrant than their background, neutrals often work in the opposite way: they anchor and calm colours which might otherwise look too strong. Here, on the other hand, the warm golden brown of the chair and the dried flowers provide the interest against the soft green wallpaper and the gently patterned fabric, which, without the rich glow of the cane, would have looked too bland. The result is peaceful and harmonious yet lively, and the cool, receding green would make a small room seem somewhat larger.

EQUAL TONES

The colours in the fabric – beiges, dove-grey, soft green and terracotta – as well as the toning plains, all have the same intensity. The neutrals act here as a good calming influence, adding depth and solidity, and the plain fabrics, used as cushions, piping and even curtain lining, would provide the finishing touch to this carefully planned scheme. Orange is always good with neutral browns and beiges and in its more muted tones it can blend into a rich brown neutral, while the blue fabric has a slightly grey cast which brings it down to the neutral level. A green fern, echoing the fabric, might be added to the scene.

SHADES AND CONTRASTS

Neutrals lend themselves to being contrasted with one another in an elegant build-up of gentle tones and textures. Lacquered cream walls can be contrasted gently with a thickly woven Berber carpet. Add furnishings of ecru corduroy, bleached linen, raw Indian silk and pale wood, and the result will be both elegant and, in its way, lively.

Yellows and violets, cerulean blues and pinks contrast well with neutrals, just as a late rose or a blue sky above lend excitement to a winter garden composed of the soft browns and beiges of branches, dry leaves and seed heads, and the gentle grey green of the grass.

Of course, the same build-up of neutral shades and textures can be contrasted much more forcibly with browns and tans, apricots and oranges or flashes of red. A scheme of this nature could be developed from the image of a steeplechase in winter: the tans and gleaming chestnuts of the horses; the tangled brown branches of the trees in the background; the browny beiges of the jumps; the stretches of water (translated into glass or marble table tops) and the bright contrasting splashes of colour from the jockeys' shirts.

Coia or rush matting is an excellent base for a combination of textured neutrals. You could use it with unbleached linen or sail-cloth upholstery juxtaposed with thick, creamy tweed, darker cream lacquer, tan suede, vertical or matchstick blinds, an old cane chair or chaise longue and an enormous choice of wall treatments, including plain cream paint or cream lacquer, rag rubbing in cream and dark cream, paper with a rag-rubbed or marbled effect, or any other form of broken paintwork.

A stroke or splash of literally any contrasting colour takes on a particular brilliance against this sort of calm but interesting background: a vase of daffodils, roses or crysanthemums, depending on the season; a plant; a few pieces of china; books; paintings or sculpture would all stand out with intensity.

Inspiration for neutral schemes can be found in a variety of places, including cities. Look at familiar scenes in the last light of day or the first light of morning, when the absence of sun devoids colours of all intensity. Examine and remember the subtleties and transmute them into gentle schemes in which you can relax and feel at peace with the world.

ABOVE Again you will notice that the textural contrasts – cane, wool, glass and steel – give all the liveliness to a completely monochrome setting. This interior is sleek and sophisticated and totally devoid of clutter. The warm cream colour scheme makes the room appear light and sunny as well as airy and spacious. The green of the plants stands out quite startlingly against the pallor of this stylish yet comfortable room.

LEFT The varying textures of honey-coloured wood, dark, shiny tiles, cane, canvas and pottery make this roomful of contrasting neutrals look warm and satisfying. The abundance of plants adds a useful freshness but appears entirely natural in this quiet, woody setting.

ABOVE A collection of drawings in simple dark wooden frames set against cream and terracotta walls are the dominant motif of this small bedroom. The quilted bedspread and short curtains, ideal for a cottage bedroom, are the only other blocks of colour, except for the green and white of flowers and the ceramic grouping. But it is peaceful, and the white marble surfaces of the bedside cabinet add just the right touch of cool simplicity. If you have a dark or north-facing bedroom, this colour scheme would make it look warmer and more welcoming.

ABOVE If the framework of a room is neutral, any pronounced shape stands out with extra intensity. In this well-proportioned room the chairs and table base assume an immediate importance, as, in a way, do the fan and the plants. The cork titles, so practical in a dining room, make an unobtrusively textured flooring. Virtually nothing detracts from the furniture and the light, gently filtering through the Venetian blind (shade).

LEFT A pair of nineteenth-century plant stands with their distinctive shapes provide the focal point in this living room with its serene colouring and charmingly green view outside. More plants on the deep window sills add extra points of contrast to the prevailing neutral shades of warm, pale mushroom walls and simple white curtains caught high and tied. Against this serenity, the few prints, and any other small flashes of colour, such as the fuchsias, stand out in a graphic way.

LEFT Polished pine vanity unit, floor and long window frames make this actually rather spare bathroom seem warm, handsome and inviting, with the plain white walls accentuating the golden shades and grainy texture of the wood. An old white painted overmantel looks good over the inset basins (sinks), and the only contrasts are the fresh blue and white blinds (shades) and the deep blue towels, apart, that is, from the outside view which is nicely reflected in the big mirror.

ABOVE LEFT It does not take much to enliven a basically neutral space – here both walls and floor have the colour of bleached sand. An old chair, a table, a basket and an off-white shawl, all with differing textures and subtly coloured surfaces, manage to make this small hallway look thoroughly relaxed and interesting. Admittedly there is the addition of a hat, a pitcher and a painting, but they, too, are very simply coloured in straw, pale terracotta and burnt orange.

ABOVE Well-arranged dressers (hutches) are always worth gazing at, since the wood supports are used to provide a gentle frame for the goods within. In this case the generous shelves are white-painted under a tongue-and-groove wood ceiling, and hold a nice mixture of white china and terracotta pottery, while bowls of oranges and apples provide small splashes of contrasting colour and candles softly highlight small portions of a scene which is crowded with interest.

ACCENT

Neutrals are not generally used to provide accents in the strictest sense. If anything, they need to be accented themselves. Nevertheless, they perform an invaluable service in anchoring and calming or pulling together other more intense colours. Almost any composition, whether in nature or painting, has its grounding strokes of cream, beige or brown. The most brilliant of southern scenes shimmering under a burnished blue sky has its dusty road. The most dazzling herbaceous border has its patches of earth. A mostly red room would be unsettling without the calming influence of, for example, a beige carpet, or at least a hint of beige or cream, just as thick rich cream both mellows and enriches the flavour of fresh raspberries or strawberries.

Because neutrals are obvious background colours, this does not mean that they need to be present in large expanses to exert their calming influence: a soft stony beige can give purpose and depth to a colourful print or design, just as an old stone wall acts as a prop for a rambling rose, a honeysuckle, a wistaria or a clematis. Only glimpses of wall may be visible through the riot of flowers and leaves but the stone imparts an air of sheltering and protective solidity to the fragile garden scene.

In a similar way, a roomful of pastels – apricots, peaches, pistachio greens and honeysuckle yellows – is made much more settled with the accent of a sofa or a pair of chairs in a quiet neutral cream. A polished wood floor provides the perfect setting for a richly coloured Persian rug, just as the dark glow of oak or mahogany, or the lighter shades of elm or yew, prevent colourful chintzes from becoming cloyingly sweet.

There is no colour in nature that does not on occasion benefit from a neutral to set it off. The gaudiest, glossiest butterfly has its occasional smudge of browny beige. The light bright greens of the leaves and the hazy clouds of bluebells in a woodland scene in late spring need the contrast of the brown trunks of trees, just as earlier in the year the dark expanses of earth accentuate the beauty and promise of the first flowers of the season.

ABOVE The dark brown of the curtain pole and rings, along with the tile floor, provide the accents in another very white space. If the floor, too, had been white, the room could have seemed very insubstantial indeed. As it is, these few neutrals anchor and delineate the space with ease. The textured pattern of the lace also helps to add depth and interest, as does the plant.

LEFT White walls and ceiling, off-white stone floor, and a good deal of white furniture make the central group of mirror, small pine desk and elongated chair seem very much the focal point of this pristine space. And, indeed, the neutral, woody colours do provide a kind of solidity against the expanse of white, linking it with the trees, the sun-grazed green and long view seen through the cool and unadorned windows.

ABOVE In this long room, where the floor-to-ceiling windows at the far end are a marvellous source of natural light, the accents are provided by the inset bookshelves, paintings and the rush basket containing the Kentia palm, together with glimpses of the polished wooden floor. All this adds solidity to the framework of walls and ceiling surrounding the island of dining table and chairs set on the rug. The floor is a striking feature in itself and adds much warmth and a glowing reflective surface to this cool room.

RIGHT The golden Afghan rug, coia matting and pine side table and mirror, again in neutrals, provide as much accent colour in this peaceful little hallway as the red lacquered seventeenth-century Venetian chair by the door and the blue and white pot, adding the essential touch of warmth and texture needed to offset the stark simplicity of the plain white walls. Although this space is fairly narrow, it looks both light and spacious, and the neutral matting gives definition to the room.

EQUAL TONES

Within the neutral range, camel and grey go particularly well together, as do soft coffee and cream, but they can also form beautiful combinations with other colours: camel goes with soft ultramarine, dove grey goes with rose, coffee goes with apricot and cream harmonizes delightfully with rose.

Using a neutral as an equal tone with another colour will always make the latter seem more peaceful and, conversely, the neutral will become more lively. In other words, the neutral is always the balancer, in decorative schemes as in nature, and this applies both to the room as a whole and to wallpaper and fabric designs. It is very important to pay just as much attention to the balance of colours in the designs as to the harmony of the overall scheme.

As always, you can look to nature for inspiration: a group of horses in an autumnal field, for example, would be particularly attractive, with the chestnuts of their coats allying with the browns, golds and crimsons of the trees, the leaf-strewn grass and the pale grey blue of the sky. The same golden tones could be repeated in a room with a polished wood floor, furniture in walnut and light old mahogany, old cane and perhaps even marquetry. Upholstery could be in ecru and a deep rose, and possibly in leather. Window treatments could range from wood shutters to a fabric in any of the golden tones or in rose and green. Whatever the choice, the feeling would remain the same.

A similar theme could be adapted from the Scottish highlands in autumn, with the rich golden brown of the bracken, the expanses of pinkish purple heather, the clear blue of the sky reflected in a loch, the outcroppings of rock and the off-white dots of sheep in the distance.

Alternatively, you could return again to the theme of the sea, with an image of bleached white sand, the scrub of blue green and purply grass that grows by the shore, thrown-up driftwood and the foam-flecked green blue of the water. Here you would have a calm room of bleached browns, creams and off-whites; glass-topped tables and blue-green prints, with a healthy selection of greenery warmed with touches of rose. There is almost no scene in nature that cannot be adapted and reproduced in textiles, paints, and furnishings.

LEFT The bleached sand, pale rose, blue and green are used throughout this room in wallpaper, festoon blind (shade), upholstery fabric and tablecloth in various co-ordinating designs. No colour is more dominant than the others, but the whole scheme of muted pastels is given a lift by the warm glow of the natural wood floor and window frame.

RIGHT All of the colours in this log cabin quilt are blended together with a nice equality; there is nothing to jar the eye or distract from the pleasant, peaceful quality of this quiet bedroom, which is as it should be. The colours, in fact, are like an abstracted beach scene with blues and sands and bleached browns.

ABOVE In this picture, a gentle fabric design in camels, greys and soft blue green blends harmoniously with the creamy cushion (pillow), cream and grey striped walls and the dappled browns and beiges of the marble mantelpiece and the ribbed wool throw. The range of colours is limited but nicely balanced, and permits a multitude of objects – books, vases, pots, candlesticks, small trays, a plant and some dried flowers – to be displayed in one small corner without producing a distractingly busy effect.

RIGHT Differing textures of walls, carpet and upholstery, though subtle, add as much interest to this peaceful room as the gentle colours of the prints, cushions (pillows), the pink and white stripe of the window seat, the rose trim to the blinds (shades) and the fresh roses on the table. All tones seem equal in their way, a gentle unity which is subtly emphasized by the pink piping round the grey scatter cushion (pillow).

BLACK & WHITE

ELEGANT, SOPHISTICATED, DRAMATIC, STYLISH, PURE

Strictly speaking, black and white come at either end of the neutrals range and are not really colours at all. Black is in fact colourless from the absence or complete absorption of all light, while white is a blend of all the colours of the rainbow in a perfect balance. White mixed with black produces a whole series of greys which link these two implacable opposites.

As a figure of speech, it is said of people who hold strong opinions that they see things in black and white, while others of a more liberal frame of mind think more in terms of grey.

On its own, black can have the sophistication of formal evening wear, or it can be a symbol of death in the West, while white stands for purity and weddings, Chinese funerals and Indian widowhood. Together, however, they make a dramatic duo: black cloak and shining dagger; the sable and argent of heraldry; the microcosmic battles of the chessboard, or the white deserts and black tents of the nomads. Many great photographers, such as Cecil Beaton or Bill Brandt, preferred black and white photographs because they pinpoint character better than colour images, which offer too many visual distractions.

Black and white tends to make a dramatic

combination in nature also: herds of zebra galloping across the African plains; killer whales; penguins; or on a larger scale there are glaciers with deep black chasms.

Black stones and minerals are much sought after. Obsidian is a luscious satiny black which takes its name from the volcanic glass discovered, according to Pliny, by the Roman traveller Obsidius. Centuries later, during the Napoleonic campaigns in Egypt, obsidian was rediscovered and came into fashion in France for all manner of household goods. Jet is another glossy, lustrous black, named after the hard coal which the Victorians loved to use for jewellery, buttons and trimmings.

The deep reddish black of ebony wood was much favoured for eighteenth-century English furniture and for French furniture at the start of the previous century. Ebony was often inlaid with mother of pearl in the oriental manner, an effect which the Victorians imitated with their papier mâché furniture.

If black lends elegance and a touch of the exotic to a scheme, white symbolizes innocence and freshness. But white can also be joyful, elegant and luxurious: white furniture gives a feeling of sunny days; white marble evokes the images of ruined temples, while white-on-white rooms seem the ultimate in luxury.

SHADES AND CONTRASTS

Black and white are ultimate opposites, with all the shades of grey in between to give liveliness and subtlety and to provide an invariably excellent background for judicious splashes of colour. In this setting, the grey wallpaper is softened by the greys mixed with pastels of the lavish fabric, while the black chair, like the gaunt outlines of a tree in a winter landscape, provides an unexpected focal point. The combination of black with soft greys and pastels often – as here – works well, providing a useful counterpoint to the gentleness of the other colours.

ACCENT

A touch of black in a room, no matter what the colour scheme, acts in the same way as a punctuation mark in writing. Here, the clean, gently curving lines of the chair and the smooth, simple shape of the black vase, both emphasize and, in a way, calm the rather pyrotechnic hues of the fabric. White, set against this striking mass of colour, would not be nearly so effective, and note that the black of both the chair and the vase is not a strong glossy black, which might compete too fiercely with the reds and tans, but an off-black, more of a very deep charcoal grey, like dark branches seen against autumn colours.

EQUAL TONES

Equal tones of grey and yellow are both fashionable and sophisticated and would look happily at home in an urban setting. The yellow fabric could be used for curtains, with grey tie-backs, and the grey fabric for upholstery, perhaps with yellow piping and cushions (pillows) for a co-ordinated effect. A carpet in soft greens and greys would add another gentle tone to this quiet, well-balanced scheme. Grey can often act as an anchor for a scheme based on a mixture of equal tones because it tends to soften and level other colours without destroying their impact, as here where the grey softens the yellow but the general effect remains warm.

SHADES AND CONTRASTS

Black, white and all shades of grey can be used to darken or lighten colours by placement as much as by mixing the pigments. For example, black set by red will make the red seem darker, whereas white will make it appear lighter and brighter, and the same sort of effect is achieved with all brilliant colours.

Set a floral print against a black background and it will instantly seem more sophisticated: a white background will both lighten and freshen the colours. White in a pastel room will make the place seem cooler and more spacious. Use white woodwork, a bleached floor and white flowers in a warm toned room and the colours will appear fresh as well as warm.

Just as there are varying shades of other colours, so there are differing tones of black and white. Think of blackberries, blackcurrants, grapes, caviar, pickled walnuts, coal, charcoal, black marble, black patent leather, ebony and soot and you will recognize the enormous range of shades and textures of not-so-solid black. True black is absence of colour, but for decorating purposes, of course, all blacks are in fact a blend of colours which achieve this effect. Black paints tend to have a bluish, reddish or brownish tinge, and this can be accentuated and used to add to the atmosphere of a scheme, recreating the velvety blue black of night or the brownish black of sheltering caves.

Equally, there are numerous whites: the greeny white of apple flesh, the pink-tinged white of roses, the creamy white of ivory and sheepskin rugs, the blue white of marble and the clean whites of blue eyes and porcelain. If you were designing a white-on-white room, like that of Elsie de Wolf, leader of fashion in the 1930s, you could make an interesting play on the textures and surfaces, creating a room as lively in its subtle way as a roomful of colour.

Grey, of course, covers an enormous range of shades and tones, from the grey of doves and wisps of mist to the lustrous grey of black pearls or the sober grey of city suiting. Moreover, the addition of grey to almost any colour can bring down some of the most positive shades to a near neutral status. The grey green of firs, for example, or of Chinese celadon can be used for subtle contrast in beige or grey-green neutral rooms.

LEFT The tiled border at the top of the splendid porcelain stove, the plants, the painting, the polished brass and the bare floor boards are the only colours in this otherwise white room, but the contrasts and the balance are very satisfactory and the room is full of airiness and quiet charm. This subtle colour scheme would work equally well in any room regardless of its aspect for there is just enough colour to give visual warmth even without sunlight.

ABOVE In a basically all-white room, any colours stand out with vivid intensity and become doubly noticeable by benefit of their unsullied and stunning white background. In this case the blue of the carpet in the alcove is given added depth and richness, the gold frame of the painting draws the eye, and the pinks and lilacs of the flowers and the cushions (pillows) are given a bright, jewel-like quality not normally associated with pastel shades.

ABOVE This bathroom is striped with grey marble slips and white tiles and takes full advantage of the sloping ceiling and deep wall recess and window embrasure. Note the trefoil windows above the bath, the details of the darker grey towel and the polished chrome of the old-fashioned heated towel rail, all set against a gleaming wood floor, which adds a touch of warmth to a predominantly cool room. The general impression is of a very much larger space.

ABOVE The very pale beige of the carpet, the bronze lamp and the creamy yellow flowers make a restful contrast to the white, as does the black table and all the greenery, within and without.

LEFT A series of neatly hung black and yellow Albers, a glass vase of brilliant yellow tulips and a couple of ashtrays along with the large plant make excellent contrasts against the white, grey and black in this spare and disciplined minimalist room, with its total absence of clutter and extraneous objects.

ACCENT

Black and white are natural accents, delineators, outliners. The Egyptians outlined their frescos in black vegetable dyes or in a black pigment made from crushed bones. Today, black added to a design or painting in primary colours sets the work in sharper focus, while black ink will give a pencil and wash drawing altogether more depth and life. Add a plain or a black and white tiled floor to a white room and you will achieve the same graphic quality. Similarly, touches of black in the form of a lamp or a black lacquered chair or table, will give substance and add elegance to a pastel room.

White accents, as has already been mentioned, impart instant freshness to rooms as they do to clothes. Add white highlights to a basically apricot, green, blue, pink or red room and the space is immediately freshened and livened. The elaborate cornices, mouldings and plasterwork of houses from the seventeenth to nineteenth centuries were included for just this reason, to stop the eye and relieve large areas of colour. The same effect can be achieved in a more modest way by white painted woodwork, coves and skirting boards (baseboards). White upholstery in, for example, a room with yellow or apricot walls will make even the gloomiest space seem lighter and more airy.

White buildings make the sky seem bluer, just as white daisies intensify the green of a lawn. White spots on a dark ground give depth to a fabric, as do white stripes, checks or squares, while white rugs on a dark floor add extra depth and dimension.

Silver is a subtler but equally useful accent. In a neutral room, tubular chairs or a polished metal edge round table tops add to the combination of tones and textures, while silver with blue, for example silver picture frames against soft blue walls, is as much of a natural for romantics as moonlight on water. Similarly, in a room of soft warm pinks and peaches and floral chintzes, touches of silver gently reflecting the colours will evoke the image of a small pool in a summery garden.

Greys generally need to be accented, but used against white, cream or camel they provide their own focal point. Add shiny grey chairs to a camel painted living room, or paint window frames, doors and skirting boards (baseboards) a gentle grey to contrast with white painted walls in any room in the house. The effect of this will be to add an accent colour so gentle and subtle that the mind is almost subconsciously aware of its existence.

ABOVE Here, the black painted spiral staircase adds the strong accent to this space as well as acting as a sculptural room divider.

RIGHT Striking black beams form the accent as well as much of the pattern in this terracotta tiled room with its regiment of plants. Beams are matched by the black and white rug thrown over the sofa. Note, too, how the black divisions of the windows and the beams with the plaster removed from in between them, act as a skeletal space divider. In fact, the black has been used to delineate and outline the white walls and ceiling.

RIGHT Black is a dramatic accent, and this is a very deliberate black and white scheme, with the effect of the black chairs, the black lamp with its black telephone wire cord and the dark-rimmed marble table top echoed by the elaborate railings of the balcony outside the long windows. In this very restrained setting, anything colourful on the table stands out with almost graphic intensity against the deliberate and subdued simplicity of the room. This colour scheme would be best suited to a room where the light is soft – bright sunshine might make the composition seem too harsh.

ABOVE This intricate white mirror frame, formed from entwined branches, is matched by the white lamp shades, dresser, ceramics and dazzling white orchid plant to form an interesting still life against the grey green of the wall behind. Note how the lamp bases echo this colour and how the mirror reflects it. The general effect is like Arctic conditions around a great frozen waste of water and is very dramatic with its strong white play of shapes and differing textures contrasting beautifully with the deep, soothing green of the walls.

EQUAL TONES

Black and white together is an unbeatable combination with a long history including the black and white marble floors of palaces and the blackened beams and whitewashed walls of old cottages. Since they lie at either end of the neutral range, however, black and white cannot really be used as equal tones with other colours, although, as discussed earlier in this chapter, they can influence the tone of other colours to a marked extent.

Unlike the extremes of black and white, greys blend beautifully with almost every colour you could think of. In this era, grey has become very fashionable and is called 'today's beige' by fashion consultants. In fact, it is just as restful as the perennial beige and camel and works just as well alongside these as it does on its own with white. A mixture of grey, white and camel – perhaps grey flannel walls, camel carpet, white painted furniture and bedspread and camel curtains – is especially restful in a bedroom and looks particularly good when accented with blue and white china and a bunch of lilac or irises, or a pink azalea.

Grey also has a natural affinity with rose, and a soft grey with a deep soft rose evokes the calm and peaceful atmosphere of a summer evening, with the last rays of the sun falling on an old stone wall. An unusual combination for a dining room is deep rose walls, rose and grey curtains, grey mouldings and a bleached floor stained pale grey.

Another pleasing grey combination, again reminiscent of sunset, is soft dove grey with lilac and white, cheered up with roses and rose framed prints.

Artists often choose grey rather than white paper for drawings and pastels because it imparts a background warmth and depth without detracting from the colours or lines. In room schemes, grey blends with and enriches pastel shades, giving pale yellows, for example, a luminous quality like rays of sunlight shining through gentle misty clouds. Similarly, although grey cannot be in any way classed as an equal tone with bright primary shades, it does have the effect of softening rather than accenting such colours and making them, perhaps, more restful to live with.

LEFT In this splendidly simple tiled bathroom the deep grey of the towels and bathmat hold equal precedence with the green of the *Ficus benjamina* and look as sculptural in their way as the old bath. Amid this sort of simplicity, the square tiles with their faint grey grouting stand out like graph paper.

RIGHT The dark greys and reds of the abstract patterns in upholstery and cushions (pillows) in this room seem to pack almost as much punch as the black of the screen and the handsome black vases in front of the charcoal painting. But then the ox blood pots and the deep ochre jar stand on much the same equal tones as the other cushions (pillows) and the rug on the deep ochre carpet. The mix of colours is well chosen.

BELOW Black and white carry equal importance in this modern kitchen. A black-trimmed stove is teamed with a black extractor hood and backed onto a neat black and white unit to serve as a room divider between kitchen and eating areas. The white floor with black diamond tiles give unity to the whole area. Against all the white the forest of greenery introduces life and a bit of colour. In spite of the stark colour scheme, the room looks warm due to its sunny aspect.

BELOW Black slatted frames are in-filled with graphic black and white stripped upholstery to form an interplay of strong lines in this sitting room. The same sort of interplay is repeated with the black-painted radiator, the strongly figured marble mantelpiece and the severe black frames, all set above a neat white tiled floor. The effect is a modern, sleek sophistication suitable for a large town house: an ideal background for a modern art collection.

RIGHT A very dramatic, very graphic bathroom/exercise room, where the thin vertical black lines of the tiles are played off against the thin horizontal lines of the Venetian blinds (shades), and strong yellow vies with the black and white and the green of the plants for attention. The result is certainly striking although the deep grey of the towels and the odd note of pink act as a sort of buffer for the strength of all the other shapes, colours and textures.

DATA FILE

WALLS

As we all know, walls can either be painted, papered, or covered with fabric, but it is easy to forget that within these broad categories there are literally dozens of different treatments and methods, with effects which range from combating the light in a room, or the lack of it, and disguising faults such as bad proportions to producing a whole series of varying effects and illusions. As the late Basil Ionides wrote in his classic book *Colour and Interior Decoration*, published in the 1920s: 'Never believe that anything is impossible in painting or papering. With ingenuity one can achieve almost any result.'

The Many Uses of Paint

In general, paint is the least expensive way of transforming a room: but there can be infinitely more to painting than simply applying another coat of colour to a given space. On the simplest level, paint can be used to change the aspect of a room: if it faces north, cheerful light-giving colours like rose, yellow and apricot should be chosen; if it is dark, bright colours are best. If the room is very light, pale, delicate colours can be used.

There are various visual tricks which appear to alter the proportions of a room. For example, you can make a room that looks low seem higher by painting the ceiling a paler colour than the walls and by emphasizing vertical lines in woodwork, such as doors and window frames.

Another way of adding to the apparent height of a room is to divide the walls into panels, keeping the proportions of these tall and narrow. This can be done with applied mouldings. If you paint the areas inside the mouldings a slightly darker shade than the rest of the walls, they will appear recessed.

A room which seems too high can be made to look lower by painting the ceiling a darker colour than the walls, particularly if you use a glossy paint, and by adding a dado at chair-back height, dividing the wall horizontally into two sections. This can be achieved most easily by superimposing pieces of moulding, painted to match the other woodwork in the room, and then painting the lower section of the wall in a subtly contrasting colour.

If you are good at painting, or have a good painter, you can achieve the same effect by painting the walls in two sections, with a straight contrast at dado level and then covering the joint with a top stripe painted to match the woodwork. If you have a *trompe l'oeil* or illusionist painter conveniently to hand, you could even paint in a chair rail or dado moulding.

Spaces which might appear flat and lacking in interest can be banded or delineated with paint. Keep a simple background colour and paint skirting boards (baseboards) and woodwork in a contrasting shade: white walls and brilliant yellow woodwork is a particularly effective combination. If there are no mouldings between walls and ceiling, you can either add a cornice or cove, or you can achieve the same sort of division with a contrasting band of colour painted immediately under the ceiling.

Equally, you could paint the woodwork the same light colour as the walls and then make a contrasting stripe around doors and windows and down corners. Draw the shapes first with great precision and only fill in the shapes with paint when you are satisfied that all the stripes are straight and of the same width, or the effect will look amateurish and messy.

If a room has a number of eyesores like a confusion of pipes, off-centre doors and windows or skirting boards (baseboards) that are too deep or too narrow, these can be disguised by painting the whole room in one colour. Ideally, this should be a warm dark colour which can be crisped up with a pale carpet and furnishings.

Sometimes, of course, you can take exactly the opposite tack and make the pipes and other extrusions into a positive sculptural virtue by painting them to contrast with the walls, for example using green, yellow or red against white walls.

Stencilling

A stencilled border above the skirting board (baseboard) or below the ceiling, or both, is a useful way to enliven and give character to a room. You can buy good stencil kits at art shops and some stationers, or you can make your own stencils. Inspiration for the latter might come from the curtain or upholstery fabric chosen for the room, or from a carpet, rug or tile. Whether you use a kit or make your own stencil (the method shown in the box uses one stencil for all colours), you will get a decorative effect for a fraction of the cost of wallpaper. One point to note, however, is that the simplest designs work the best, since the whole point of stencilling is the repetition of a simple motif.

Stencilled border

To paint with a stencil you will need artists' acrylic paints in the desired colours, masking tape, sponges cut into small pieces, fine artists' brushes for touching up and adding details, paper cups or plates to use as palettes, polyurethane varnish and, of course, a stencil.

The first step is to mix the paints to the colours you want, since artists' acrylics are not available in muted or subtle shades. Do not thin the paint or it will run under the stencil and spoil your design.

Next, stick the stencil to the wall with masking tape. If you are afraid that the sticky backing may damage your newly decorated walls when the tape is removed, simply stick the tape to your hand or arm a few times to reduce the adhesive effect.

The paint is applied to the cut-out areas with small sponges. Dip a small piece of sponge into one colour of paint; get rid of the excess paint by dabbing it vigorously up and down on a clean portion of the plate or cup, and then dab the paint onto the wall through the hole in the stencil.

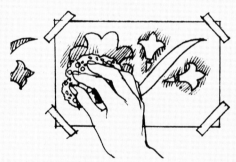

Applying paint with sponge

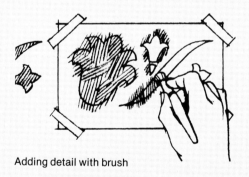

Adding detail with brush

Paint all the areas in one colour at one time and choose small bits of sponge for very small areas. Very thin lines like stems, stamens or the antennae of butterflies can be left and stroked in with a brush later.

When all the holes have been filled in, carefully untape the stencil and lift it off, taking care not to let it drag.

Use a brush to fill in any missing details and correct mistakes, then move on to the next repeat, making sure that you keep the repeats an equal distance apart and on a straight line.

Finally, when the wall is completely dry, add a coat of polyurethane varnish with a roller. This will make the wall washable and preserve the stencilling.

Making a stencil

You will need the following:
    Cráyons and pencil
    Tracing paper
    A sheet of acetate
    Craft knife
    Masking tape

Make a full-scale drawing of the chosen motif (most photocopy agencies will enlarge or reduce images for you if necessary). Trace the motif, isolating the various parts of the design such as trunks or stems, leaves, fruit or petals, and outlining them so that they fit together but do not quite join up.

When you have made your tracing, use it to make several copies of the design and then colour these in with crayons, experimenting with different colour combinations until you have one which seems satisfactory.

Next, place the sheet of acetate over your design, securing it with masking tape. Position the acetate so that its top or bottom edge can align with the ceiling or skirting board (baseboard) when you are using the finished stencil. Trace the motif on the acetate.

Remove the tracing paper and, using a craft knife, cut out the different elements of the motif. You will get a smoother edge if you turn the acetate round as you cut rather than lifting up the knife. Once the design is cut, the stencil is ready.

Glaze

The days when sophisticated techniques such as glazing, rag rubbing, dragging and stippling were left to the top decorators have gone. There is a universal fascination with the wall finishes which can be achieved both

by conventional and unconventional methods, and it is in fact much easier to get truly beautiful colours – a clear apricot, for example, or the warm yellow tinged with rose of a papaya – with a two- or three-toned approach than it is with solid colours. This, of course, is a thesis with which artists, as opposed to house painters, have been experimenting for centuries.

The common denominator of most of these decorative finishes is a glaze. This is a transparent, ready-mixed oil coat, which can be tinted and then used with effects such as rag rubbing (unlike polyurethane varnish, which is simply a clear, hard protective coating). Any wall to which glaze is applied will come out with a richness and depth of colour which could never otherwise be achieved. If the glaze is tinted with the same sort of colour as the base coat, the finish will be a deeper and more transluscent version of that particular tone. If the glaze and the base coats are in different colour groups but are of the same intensity, or if the glazing coat is somewhat darker than the base coat, you will get some marvellously subtle results. Dark green over a medium green will turn your walls a rich jade. A Sienna brown glaze over a deep green base will produce a glowing terracotta.

Glaze can be bought from paint stores and half a litre covers approximately 11 square metres (one pint/2 cups for 120 square feet). It normally requires rather less glaze than paint to cover the same area since the glaze will be thinned with white spirit (mineral spirits) to the easiest consistency for working.

The simplest way to tint a glaze is to let the paint store do it for you, but it is not always easy to get exactly the right shade this way. If you want to tint the glaze yourself, squeeze a length of artists' oil paint or tinting colour into an old saucepan or a foil pie tin then stir in several tablespoons of white spirit (mineral spirits). Mix this very thoroughly and then add about a cup of the glaze and mix again. Test the mixture on the wall or a board: it can easily be wiped off if you are not satisifed. Continue to experiment until you have the colour you want, but never mix the tint straight into the glaze because it will be difficult to homogenize.

Whichever paint effect you finally choose, it is absolutely vital to make sure that walls, ceiling and woodwork are in good condition before you start, otherwise your efforts will be sadly short-lived. If there are any major problems with damp, staining or deep fissures in the plaster, the underlying problems must be dealt with first. If there are only surface blemishes, you will still have to ensure that any loose paint is removed, cracks are filled in and smoothed over and plaster is sanded smooth. End up by washing the walls all over with a solution of warm water and a bit of ammonia. Only after this is the surface well prepared.

One final word of warning: glaze must be painted onto a base which has already been given a coat, preferably two coats, of an oil-based (alkyd) eggshell or semi-gloss ground in order to achieve a smooth finish. Never use emulsion (latex) paint as this will simply absorb the glaze and the effect will be ruined.

The simplest form of glazing is to apply a tinted glaze over an opaque, oil-based (alkyd) ground coat. Apply the glaze evenly, avoiding untidy drips and runs. Whichever colour you choose, you will end up with highly pleasing transparent depths.

Once the walls have been glazed in this manner or in any of the ways, such as rag rubbing, described below, you can give them a seal coat or two of polyurethane varnish. This will give them a handsome sheen and protect the finish, though it tends to darken the tone a little. Decide whether you want polyurethane with a matt, semi-gloss or gloss finish, then apply it with a roller. Finish by brushing the coat with a large brush or a cheap foam pad to get rid of the small bubbles which inevitably collect. If you omit this last step, the bubbles might harden and dry, not only ruining the whole effect, but doing so in perpetuity. Always allow 24 hours between coats for the varnish to dry.

Stippling

This is an attractive effect which is achieved by applying the glaze to walls and woodwork with a brush with a broad, blunt cut (you can use a shoe brush or a soft scrubbing brush if you do not want to buy a special stippling brush). The walls are painted in a white or light-coloured base coat. When they have dried, the glaze is first painted on with an ordinary brush and then worked over with the stippling brush before it has had a chance to dry. The finish should have a slightly grainy, freckled or mottled effect, with the base coat showing through the glaze. Because the technique is somewhat laborious, it is best if two people can work together: one to apply the paint and the other to follow with the stippling brush.

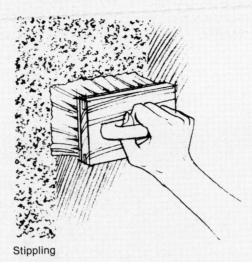
Stippling

Dragging

This is another glaze effect, rather similar to stippling in method, but resulting in a softly textured wall with fine irregular vertical striations, which tend to make rooms look larger and higher.

Dragging is achieved by applying a coat of a paint in a light colour to the wall and allowing it to dry, then covering this with a darker-tinted glaze and, before the glaze has dried, 'dragging' it by brushing it down with a wide, dry brush. If you plan to drag many rooms, it is worth while buying a special dragging brush, with long, flexible bristles. A standard 12.5cm (5in) paintbrush, however, will work quite well, though you will have to move quickly since it will not cover such a wide surface and the glaze must remain wet during dragging.

Woodwork, such as skirting boards (baseboards), doors and window frames, also look good with a dragged finish.

Dragging

Rag rubbing

Rag rubbbing is a much more free-flowing version of stippling and can be done quite easily by one person alone. After the base coat has dried, the glaze is painted on. Before it is dry, take a bunch of rags, which should first have been wetted in turpentine or white spirit (mineral spirits), and either dab it on the glaze with one hand or, making a bundle of the rags, roll it over the glaze. The rags should be rinsed out in spirit from time to time so that they do not get clogged up with glaze. It is wise to finish up with a protective coat or two of polyurethane.

Rag rubbing

Effective rag-rubbed combinations include rosy glazes over creamy yellow; pinky lilac over white, or mint green over creamy white. You will get different textures depending on whether you use cheesecloth, hessian (burlap) or old sheeting.

Lacquering

Proper lacquering, as done in the Far East, is a very slow job, but as long as you have good smooth walls you can achieve several attractive approximations, using either polyurethane varnish or a combination of glaze and varnish.

The simplest method is to apply a couple of coats of clear, thinned down gloss or semi-gloss polyurethane over two or three coats of oil-based (alkyd) flat or eggshell paint. The base coats do not have to be glass smooth because the varnish fills in cracks and holes.

Another method is to paint a series of tinted glazes over a base coat, leaving ample time for them to dry in between, and then to finish with a protective coat of polyurethane. This gives a good-looking pearlized effect.

A third way is to tint the glaze with

progressively lighter shades of the same colour between coats, building up several layers. Again, this should be finished with a coat or two of polyurethane.

Wallpaper

Wallpaper is an excellent disguiser, hiding uneven or cracked surfaces and giving an instant change of style to a room. Before you make your choice from the enormous range of papers available, however, it is important to make sure that the walls are sound, though they do not need to be as immaculate as they would for a painted finish.

Covering defects
If your walls are not perfect, lining paper can be a great help. Choose a heavy type and hang it in horizontal strips, taking care to butt up the edges so that each piece lies exactly edge to edge with the next.

The best lining, if you can get it, is the canvas lining which was originally designed for use under brocades and tapestries. This hides a multitude of sins and can even be used by itself if it is sized, painted and varnished.

Embossed papers are another good way of concealing bad walls. Some of these are made from cotton fibre embossed with a pattern while others are made from layers of linseed oil welded to a backing paper and embossed with textures like hessian (burlap) or tiles. Both types should be painted.

Choosing a paper
The choice of paper will depend partly on the effect which you wish to achieve and partly on the use of the room. Vinyl wallcoverings, for example, are ideal for bathrooms, shower rooms, kitchens or playrooms because they are waterproof and are tougher than ordinary washable wallpapers.

Flock wallpapers, on the other hand, like embossed papers, provide a perfect background for antiques and eclectic furnishings.

If you want a particularly pretty, cottage-style room, then you could use one of the many beautifully drawn florals, choosing a scale to suit the proportions of your room.

If you need to make a space seem larger, a geometric design on a white or shiny ground, for example foil, will give a sense of perspective, so that the eye is drawn out; or one of the miniprints with a matching fabric, and possibly a matching or contrasting border, has the same effect in a tiny room.

Co-ordinating mini-print paper and fabrics give a sense of perspective and space

The new paint effect papers can look almost indistinguishable from the real thing, especially if they are given a gleaming coat of polyurethane varnish. Use these, or the plain-coloured or marble papers with some of the handsome friezes and borders available, which are often printed specially to co-ordinate with them.

Borders
Borders can be used in a number of different ways apart from their use as an edging to a co-ordinating paper. One idea is to use them as panels: choose borders which are the same colour but a different shade from the walls. The two shades must not be too different, however, just sufficiently different to make the panels appear to be recessed. If they are too far apart in colouring, there will be no illusion, only irritation.

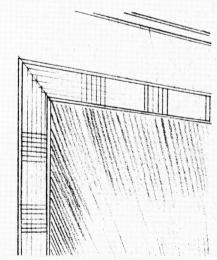

Using borders to make panels

Borders can also be used to form a false dado and, of course, to delineate doors, windows, skirting boards (baseboards) and mouldings. Unfortunately they tend to be rather expensive. One way round this is to look out for papers with a linear design or a similar pattern which can be cut up into long strips and pasted on as a border.

Fabric

In general, wall fabrics are more expensive than papers, but they neaten up mediocre proportions and cover imperfections rather more efficiently than papers. In addition, they have good sound and insulating properties and will last for years, long after paint has become chipped and discoloured and paper faded and dirty. They can be sprayed for protection against undue dirt and spot cleaned. They are also more fire retardant than most papers and, all in all, pay for themselves over and over again.

Fabrics also have the advantage of adding texture to your walls without the distraction of pattern, and there is now a wide choice available, ranging from felt, hessian (burlap) and even suede through to moiré silk.

Firm fabrics
If the fabric is reasonably firm, it can be stuck right onto the wall, although it is important to check that you are using the recommended adhesive. Paste the adhesive onto the wall not the fabric, because the latter might stretch while wet and shrink on the wall.

Frayed edges can be covered with a braid or an edging, such as lengths of wood moulding which have been painted or stained.

WINDOWS

Quite apart from the treatment of a window – the decision whether to leave it alone to stand on its own merits or to put up curtains and blinds (shades), screens, louvers or shutters – do not forget the decorative potential of windows themselves.

In all the finest houses of the seventeenth and eighteenth centuries the inside shutters and embrasures of windows were decorated with a care which proves that they were not meant to be concealed by curtains. The better the house, in fact, and the better the architectural details, the less need there was for any sort of covering. Admittedly, such windows and the architraves surrounding them were invariably more beautiful than any window produced today, but there is no reason why even the most pedestrian frame in an existing building should not be imaginatively treated and titivated, as long as this fits in with the general design of the room, for it is, after all, part of the background.

Extra trims of wood can be added to make frames more substantial. Frames and surrounds can be stained to match the floor, perhaps, or painted and left to stand on their own. A window with an especially pleasing view can be treated like a painting in a frame; and with a little judicious thought, a window with or without a view can be treated as a focal point for an entire room.

It is true that it is a shame to hide the graceful proportions and frame of an old window, nevertheless the well-dressed window – whatever the dressing – adds softness to a room as well as providing an extra vehicle for colour and design, quite apart from its insulation properties.

Awkward windows

Before deciding what to do with any type of window, you should think not just about the quality of the light you get from it, the view, and the shape of the frame, but also about any problems which might be posed by the latter. How does the window open: inward, upward or outward? How should pivot, arched, French, corner and dormer windows and those with oddly-shaped tops be treated? Is there anything you should or could do to the window itself to help the proportions before you make a final choice?

If windows open inward, say in a bedroom where you need privacy, mount sheers on the windows themselves, either stretching them on expanding wire or shirring them on slim poles attached to the frame. If you decide on curtains, make sure that the track or pole reaches well to either side of the window so that the fabric does not impede the swing of the window by day. If you decide on a blind (shade), mount it above the window frame for the same reason.

If windows are set in pairs close together, treat them as a single unit, with one pair of curtains on one pole or track, drawn back at either side, or with a permanent length of fabric in between so that they seem all of a piece by day or night. If blinds (shades) are used, make sure that they are symmetrical.

A pair of windows treated as a single unit

Corner windows can be tackled in several ways: either use one curtain and loop it back with a tieback, or use a blind (shade), or fix a café curtain right onto the window.

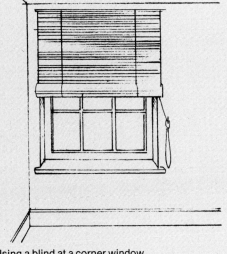

Using a blind at a corner window

Pivot windows are always a most annoying problem. Fix sheers or a double tier of café curtains onto the window, or simply make sure that any pole or track allows ample space for the curtains to be pulled clear at either side.

Sheer curtain fixed onto a pivot window

Dormer windows are best with blinds (shades) only, or else with sheers attached to the top and bottom of the frame.

A pair of corner windows set at right angles can be awkward, especially if there is very little space between them. Make sure that any poles or tracks and headings extend beyond the outside edges so that curtains can be drawn well back to the wall at either side. The only other solution to the problem is vertical louver blinds (shades) or well-fitting shutters: all other blinds would snag at the corners where they met.

Skylights can be curtained by sheers fixed directly onto the frame, or by roller, Venetian or matchstick blinds (shades) mounted on a special skylight fixture.

French windows, which are usually much prized, can also be a problem. If all the doors open, treat them as a single unit with curtains drawn to the sides, provided there is room, or with blinds (shades) set above the frames so that there is nothing to impede the door opening. If there is a single door which opens inward, fix light curtains on slim rods or on expanding wire attached to the door itself.

Arched windows are obviously handsome, so try not to conceal the arched tops at any time. Mount curtains on an arched heading which follows the line of the frame and loop them back at either side with tiebacks. (The heading would have to be mounted permanently onto the wall.) If the light or view ought not to be in any way obscured during the day, it may be necessary to forgo the arch at night. In this case, fix curtains to a rod or pole set well above the arch. It is now possible to get blinds (shades) with fixed headings which are made to fit within an arched frame, or you can have a perforated screen or panel cut to fit within the frame if the view is of no great account.

Elegant treatment for arched windows

Curtains

The length of curtains is a question of taste. Some people like to have them extravagantly sweeping the floor while others prefer them just touching. Short, sill-length curtains tend to look best in a cottage, but in other circumstances where it is not possible to hang full-length curtains – for example where there is a deep sill or a window seat or a deep radiator, and no room to extend curtains out to the side – it is generally preferable to fix a blind (shade) instead. If there is room in these situations to extend curtains to the sides, it might still be a good idea to use a blind (shade), combining it with dress curtains at either side. In this way you will not lose the window seat or the benefit of the radiator at night.

Rods, poles and tracks

Curtains can be suspended from 'invisible' rods, which display the chosen headings and nothing else; they can be suspended from tracks concealed behind pelmets or valances of one sort or another, or they can be hung from rods or poles that are intended to be seen. These can be bought in brass or wood, which may be silvered, stained, painted or covered in fabric. If only short, slim poles are necessary, wooden dowels can be bought reasonably cheaply at most hardware stores and wooden doorknobs can be screwed at either end to make effective stops. These can then be painted, stained or varnished according to taste.

If you are planning on very heavy curtains, buy brass or wooden poles with a cording set already fixed inside. This obviates the need for constant pulling and handling, which wears out the fabric.

If there is a radiator under the window and you do not want to use a conjunction of blinds (shades) and dress curtains, the most practical solution is to hang curtains by rings attached to poles. This will allow warm air to escape instead of trapping the heat behind close folds of fabric.

Curtain rods or tracks should always, if possible, be wider than the window frame so that curtains can be drawn as much to the side as possible. They come in every size, shape and variety for mounting on the ceiling or the wall, or for fitting into bays or round arches or on the underside of window frames. There are double and single rods, tension rods for lightweight curtaining, extendable rods, hinged rods for French windows and glazed doors, and ultra-slim rods which can easily be bent and shaped.

Headings

Similarly, there is an enormous variety of heading tapes available. The main types are: a standard gathering tape, for a simple gathered effect; a cartridge pleating tape, which gives a full round pleat, particularly when the pleat is filled with tissue paper; a pencil pleating tape for a neat, upright heading, and pinch or triple pleating tape, which gives gathers at regular intervals. Most tapes are stiffened and have two or three levels of pockets, so that you can hook the curtain to cover a track or to hang clear of a pole. If you have a pelmet or valance so that the top of the curtain will be concealed, special pleats are unnecessary and you can use the cheapest, unstiffened gathering tape.

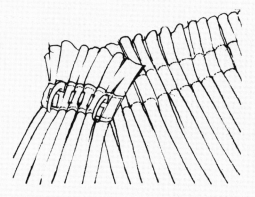

Gathered heading

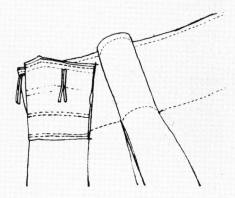

Cartridge pleating

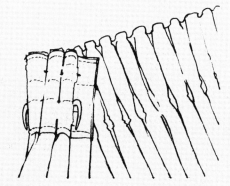

Pencil pleating

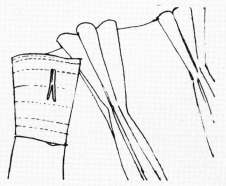

Pinch pleating

Measuring for curtains

When calculating the amount of fabric needed for curtains, it is important to start by deciding which type of tape you intend to use. The finished curtains should cover the width of your track or pole without skimping. Standard gathering tape requires fabric 1½ to 2 times the width of your track or pole (unless the fabric is very fine, more will result in a bunched-up appearance). Pencil pleats require 2¼ times fullness for heavy fabrics and 3 times fullness for very fine fabrics, while tape pinch pleats require 2 times fullness.

Add 10cm (4in) for side seams, and a further 5cm (2in) for any additional seams, assuming that you have to join widths.

The length of the curtain will depend partly on whether you are going to use the top, middle or lower pocket of your heading tape, revealing or concealing the track or pole. Add 5cm (2in) for the turning at the top (you may want more if you have a very deep tape), and 15cm (6in) for the bottom hem. If you have a pattern repeat, you must also allow for this: a general rule is to add the length of a pattern repeat to each fabric width, less one (for example, if you are using six widths of fabric you would allow for five extra pattern repeats).

An important fact to remember is that a generous amount of an inexpensive fabric will look much better than a skimped amount of a more expensive variety. Curtains should look lavish!

Pelmets and valances

Along with the return to lavish curtains has come the return of pelmets and valances and the elaborate draped heading in which a length of curtaining is twisted round a pole so that it then falls gracefully to the sides. Pelmets create a formal elegance and are used to best effect on tall windows in large rooms. They should be accompanied by full-length curtains, perhaps held back by stylish tie-backs. Valances, on the other hand, often look cheerful and informal, and are equally suitable for a cottage or a more sophisticated décor. They are also easier to make if you are not very experienced. The drawings give some idea of the enormous range of styles.

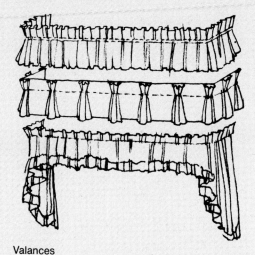

Valances

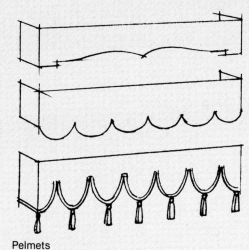

Pelmets

Blinds (Shades)

These have one great advantage over curtains: they are much cheaper. In addition, they let in more light, show off a fabric design while using less fabric than curtains, look neat and take up less space than curtains. Also, if you have attractive window frames or shutters, these could be treated as a decorative feature in their own right. There is also an infinite variety from which to choose to suit different styles of décor.

The least expensive are the paper blinds (shades) which can be bought from most oriental stores. They do not last long, but they are light, airy and useful, especially for temporary accommodation. They are excellent for giving privacy without much light loss during the day.

Next come matchstick blinds (shades), which can either be left their natural colour or spray-painted. Slightly up the scale from these are the bamboo type, followed by the various kinds of Venetian blind, ranging from quite thick slats to the narrowest possible and available in both plastic and metal. Then there are, of course, vertical louver blinds and wooden slatted ones. These have the advantage, for the most part, of being adjustable so that they can let in more or less light, but the disadvantage of tending to act as dust gatherers.

There are also an increasing number of ready-made roller blinds (shades) from which to choose, and the plain-coloured variety can always have designs painted or printed on them. It is also fairly easy to make your own roller blinds using kits available at large stores, but take advice on the correct weight and type of fabric.

Measuring for roller blinds (shades)

When measuring up for a blind it is important to decide whether it is to hang inside the window recess or outside. If it is to hang inside it must fit the glass exactly or it will hang crookedly and look skimped. If it is to hang outside the recess, the fabric should extend at least 5cm (2in) to each side of the outer edge of the window frame or it will be sucked in and look wavy.

Brackets to hold the blind (shade) can be fixed from the ceiling, just above the window frame or inside the window recess.

If possible, the width of the blind (shade) should be less than that of the fabric because seams look bulky and the extra thickness can impede the smooth action of the roller. It is possible to buy special fabric which will not fray at the sides or to use a sealer spray which will prevent ordinary fabric from fraying, but if you need to make side seams, cut them with pinking scissors or oversew them, making just one fold.

Whether the roller hangs inside or outside the recess, the fabric should be cut to a width 5cm (2in) less than the total width of the roller, including the pins. If you are making side seams, add on 2.5cm (1in) to allow for these.

The length of fabric required will be the distance from the bottom level of the roller down to the sill, or to 5cm (2in) below the sill, plus 17.5cm (7in) for hemming and fixing it to the roller.

Other types of fabric blind (shade) include Roman blinds, which concertina neatly into folds (these can now be bought ready-made in a variety of measurements); Austrian or festoon blinds, which are softer and more flouncy; pull-up curtains, which are a slightly more tailored version of the Austrian type and softer than the Roman but much less flouncy than the Austrian or festoon variety.

If blinds (shades) are used in conjunction with patterned curtains, use one of the colours in the curtain fabric to make plain blinds, or trim the blind with strips cut from the curtain fabric. If, on the other hand, the curtains are plain, you might reverse the process and have a patterned blind in co-ordinating colours.

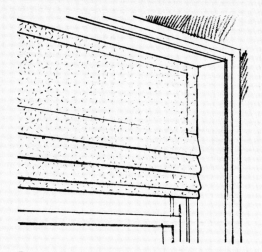

Roman blind

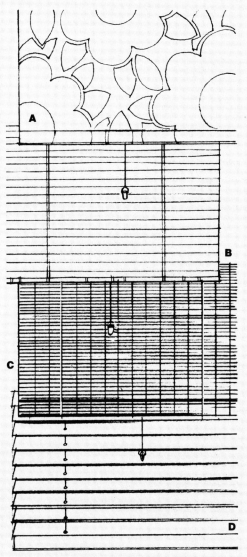

A Roller blind **B** Paper blind **C** Matchstick blind
D Venetian blind

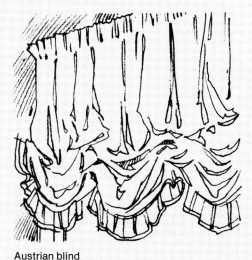

Austrian blind

Other window treatments

Shutters

You do not, of course, have to use curtains or blinds (shades): there are several alternative window treatments.

Many older houses still retain their original wood shutters and, if you are lucky enough to have these, then there is no need to add anything else. They can simply be painted with the frame or, if they are panelled, the panelling can be picked out: they can look very effective painted in two or three subtle tones, or bright contrasting colours in the style of Mondrian. Another attractive idea is to paint or stencil small designs just in the middle of the panels.

Louvered shutters can either be left in their natural wood or painted white, dark green or any other colour you might fancy.

Special effects

Windows in kitchens or bathrooms, windows which are not overlooked, or single corner windows that are of a different size and proportion to those in the rest of the room, can all be made more interesting if you put glass, or occasionally wooden, shelves across them. Mass the shelves with plants or a collection of glass or china, or with a combination of all three.

Plants used instead of curtains or blind

Hanging plants can be trailed down in front of a window that is otherwise uncovered, and evergreen creepers may be used on the outside of a window to make an otherwise dreary view appear soft and romantic. For that matter, ivy or jasmine or a similar creeper can easily be grown up an inside wall.

A tiny window can be surrounded by shelves of books and other objects as if it were in a frame, or it might be surrounded by storage closets or else left unaltered, with just a single vase or plant on the sill.

Another idea is to remove ordinary glass and replace it with panels of tinted glass which makes the outside view seem like an early aquatint, filters the light and prevents those outside from looking in. Occasionally it is possible to fit an old piece of stained glass into an existing window frame, or you might be able to commission a new piece of stained or etched glass. Alternatively, designs and paintings can be executed with special glass paint which does not wash or wear off.

Once you begin to think of a window as a frame and not just as a source of light, air and access, ideas for its treatment can become very fertile.

FLOORS

Adding up the floor area of even the smallest house or apartment can come as something of a shock, one which is scarcely tempered by the thought that whatever is put down will be walked on, sat on, lain on and generally go on taking a beating for years and years. It obviously follows that your choice should be well considered and that you should select the toughest quality available within your price range. If you decide on carpet, it should be the best you can possibly afford, even if something else has to go by the board, for cheap carpet, unless it is intended for a seldom used guest room or only needed for a limited period, will have to be replaced in a short while, making the exercise doubly expensive and inconvenient. Hard floors, too, should be both durable and good-looking, or you will get heartily sick of them. Unless you have very strong ideas, it is much better to buy a neutral flooring, whether hard or soft so that it will go with whatever colour scheme you are planning.

But before you start to think about new floors and feel worried with the anticipation of the cost, make sure that you cannot do anything about the existing surfaces. Most wood, tiles, linoleum, vinyl and even old carpet can be cleaned, bleached, stained, painted, stencilled, dyed or covered with rugs and generally brought back to shape for considerably less expense than the cost of putting down a new floor. Moreover, it might well end up looking better as well as more interesting and original.

Ideas for renovating wood floors

Underneath a good many wood floors, however much they appear to have been battered with the years, lies some beautifully grained timber longing to be admired. All that may be needed is a good sanding down to the raw wood, perhaps a stain or bleach, and the application of a transparent finish, and you will end up with an apparently brand new floor. Unfortunately some floors have worn too thin to take a sander, so it is important to take professional advice.

Sanding machines can be hired, or the job can be done by professionals. Once the floor is sanded, mop it with a solution of one part vinegar to four parts water and allow it to dry completely. You can then either stain or bleach the surface (see below) before giving it a protective layer of polyurethane.

Staining

Staining will modify the colour of a wood floor and at the same time it will bring out the grain. There are three main types of stain – oil-based, alcohol-based and water-based, – each of which gives a slightly different finish and which should be applied in different ways.

Pigmented oil stains are mixed with turpentine or white spirit (mineral spirits) and generally give the most even and glowing result; but they dry rather slowly and it is essential to wipe off the excess or it will harden into a gummy mess.

Dye stains come in a powdered form which is soluble either in water or alcohol. Water-based stains go on easily and soak into the wood quickly but tend to dry in splotches. Alcohol-based stains dry practically on the instant but are quite tricky to apply: if, for example, you overlap by accident onto an already dry area, there will be a build up of colour and, as with the water-based stains, you will get an uneven look.

Whichever stain you choose, it will look different on different types of wood, so try it out in an obscure corner of the room first. Most stains are available in various wood colours as well as green, scarlet, peacock blue, orange and yellow.

It is, of course, possible to use different colours to create patterns. The easiest way to do this – and it can be highly attractive – is to alternate the colours floorboard by floorboard.

Staining

Bleaching

A bleached wood floor can look splendidly airy and will often make a room seem much larger. Combined with rugs, it makes a most attractive floor for a living room, and is highly practical in a dining room, where a carpet might easily suffer from food stains and smells.

As with staining, you will first have to sand down and wash the floor with a solution of vinegar and water. The bleaching can generally be done with an ordinary household bleach: scrub it well in and leave it for about a quarter of an hour. When it is dry, see how it looks. If it looks light, but not as light as you had hoped, repeat the process and continue to repeat it until the desired colour has finally emerged, then rinse the floor as well as you can with water and a mop.

Unfortunately, no matter how assiduously you rinse, you will find that some of the bleach will remain and the best way to remove this residue is to give a further rinse to the floor with a half-and-half solution of vinegar and water. After this, it must be rinsed yet again with clear water. The bleaching and neutralizing is similar to the process at the hairdressers and can have just as desiccating an effect on wood as on hair. If the grain of the wood has been raised by the process, it will require one final light sanding, vacuuming and wiping before you apply at least two coats of polyurethane, remembering to allow a minimum of 24 hours between coats.

Another way of bleaching or whitening a floor is known as lightening and gives a somewhat more finished look than straight bleaching. It is also marginally quicker. In essence, the process entails painting the floor and then wiping the paint off so that it leaves a slight residue or film which is then encapsulated in a polyurethane finish, resulting in an interesting, pearly, 'antique' look. It works particularly well on pine and could look very attractive in a white-on-white room.

When lightening a floor, it is best to work with one easily manageable area at a time. Brush in flat white oil paint, wait for a few minutes, then wipe off most of the paint with a clean dry rag, working against the grain. Allow the floor to dry overnight, then seal it with the statutory two or three coats of polyurethane. If you do not want to use a plain white paint, you could try the same process with ivory, creamy white or white tinged with a grey or umber artist's oil paint.

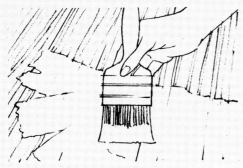

Lightening a floor: applying white paint

Wiping off paint against grain of wood

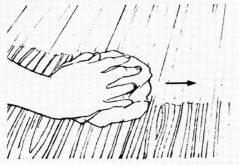

Painting

It may well be that your floors are too thin to sand, but even so it might still be possible to rescue them by simply painting them. Use deck or yacht paint or, alternatively, use ordinary paint covered with polyurethane to harden it.

If you are more ambitious for effect, you could paint the floor in a background colour of your choosing and then superimpose a stencilled pattern or border, or try variations on wall-type glazes (see pages 111–2).

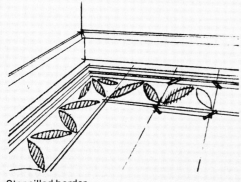

Stencilled border

Again, the surface should be finished off with a couple of coats of polyurethane, which can be renewed every year or so.

This painting technique can also be applied to old linoleum and composition tiles.

Success with polyurethane

Since virtually any revival recipe for hard floors finishes with a protective coat of polyurethane, it is worth describing the best way to use it. If you are covering a newly sanded floor, the first coat should be a sealing coat, consisting of a half-and-half solution of polyurethane diluted with white spirit (mineral spirits). When this is dry, apply at least two more coats of straight polyurethane, allowing each coat to dry for a minimum of 24 hours before you apply the next, even though the floor may feel dry to the touch.

The quickest way of applying the polyurethane is with a roller. Look out for air bubbles and go over the wet surface with a dry brush to get rid of any that appear.

A couple of days after the last coat has been applied, give the floor two coats of paste wax, buffing each coat with an electric floor polisher. This will add a soft waxy glow to the sealed floor. Remember, however, not to wax under rugs, as this can cause accidents.

Other hard floors

These range from cheap composition tiles, through linoleum, vinyl, rubber, cork and slate, to ceramic tiles and marble. Marble is now available in tile form and is therefore much lighter than used to be the case.

Even the cheapest composition tiles can be made to look quite handsome if the colours are judiciously chosen and put together

If you do not mind the hardness, quarry tiles, bricks, Mexican terracotta, French provincial tiles and old paving slabs also make beautiful kitchen and hall floors, especially for the country, where they will withstand mud, wet and dogs, as will – but less robustly – ceramic tiles and slate. This group runs from expensive to very expensive, but will last out several lifetimes.

Less permanent, but still hard-wearing, is linoleum which, like composition tiles, is coming up in the world. In fact, some of the most handsome floors around are made from inlaid linoleum, carefully cut and fitted. Cork and vinyl are excellent for children's rooms, kitchens and bathrooms. Rubber deadens the sound of childish thumps and comes in good colours.

Soft floor coverings

Carpets

If you have a really battered existing carpet, it is probably best to take it up and try to do something to the floor underneath, as suggested above. If, however, you are determined to rescue it, you can try covering the worst areas with rugs.

New carpets, as has already been pointed out, should be the best you can afford. Wool reinforced with 20 per cent nylon is used for some of the hardest wearing and best carpets on the market, because wool is comparatively dirt- and fire-resistant, takes dyes beautifully and is soft to touch. Many of the carpets made from synthetic fibres, however, are getting better all the time in colouring, design and resistance to spills, stains and dirt.

Carpet design has certainly improved enormously in recent years. Borders are becoming as popular for carpets as they are for walls, but unless you have a perfectly rectangular or square room, they will need very careful fitting.

Cheaper carpeting

If you cannot afford the more expensive ranges, have small children, or are likely to move fairly often, you might think of carpet tiles. These come in a much better range of colours nowadays, are easy to lay, and can be moved or replaced when they get worn.

Before carpeting a bathroom, think seriously of nylon carpet, because it withstands water much better than wool. One flood and wool might rot, and it will certainly smell unpleasant for weeks.

If you do not mind the hard texture underfoot, hair and wool cords look very neat and are good common denominators at ground level for a mixture of modern and old furniture. They are also extremely hardwearing and provide a good background for rugs like kelims and dhurries.

Matting

This can be extremely elegant and provides a good basis for furniture of mixed styles. It looks at home in both town and country and is relatively cheap. You can buy rush, coconut or coia (the superior form of coconut) matting, all with different weaves and textures. Rush comes in thick plaits of creamy rush and is not very practical for stairs because it can be slippery and wears badly on the edges, but it certainly looks superb elsewhere.

GLOSSARY

Accent colours
These are used in a scheme to add a bit of sparkle and variety, and are very often chosen from the opposite side of the spectrum (see Spectrum) to the main colour of the room. They are only used in small areas, for example cushions, lampshades, matts for framing prints or flowers.

Acrylic colours
This term refers to artists' acrylics, which have a water-soluble polyacrylic base and make a very versatile type of paint. They can be thinned with water to watercolour transparency, diluted with an acrylic medium for 'transparency with body', or used straight from the tube for a more opaque finish. They come in a wide range of colours and are particularly good for stencilling (see pages 110–1) as they are quick to dry.

Advancing colours
Warm colours like reds, yellows, apricots and orange, which appear to bring surfaces closer. Advancing colours may also make objects look bigger and they are useful in large rooms to bring in walls and lower ceilings. Dark shades of other colours have similar effects.

Alkyd paints
This is the American term for oil-based paints.

Architrave
Strictly speaking, this is a term from classical architecture which describes the lowest of the three primary divisions of the entablature (the part supported by a column). Nowadays the word is loosely applied to any moulding round a door or window, and such mouldings frequently borrow the profile of the architrave in the strictest sense.

Basalt
An igneous rock (one produced by solidification of the earth's internal molten magna), basalt is almost black in colour.

Bauhaus
Professor Walter Gropius founded the Bauhaus in Germany in 1919. It was a workshop in which Gropius inspired his students to create well-designed articles for mass production. His aim was to found a new rational architecture in which the archi-tect was responsible not just for the building but for all the contents of a house, from the textiles to the cutlery. Many objects produced in the Bauhaus became prototypes for mass-produced ceramics, light fitments, rugs and textiles which remain popular today.

Bleaching
In decorating, bleaching is a technique most commonly used on wooden floors. It literally means to whiten or make paler: on wooden floors some of the natural colour of the wood is removed, resulting in a clean, light and airy look (see pages 118–9).

Casein colours
Casein paints (pigments in a casein, or milk protein, base) are available only in the US. They are cheap but strong smelling, fast drying and easy to work with. The colours are strong, so only a light coat is needed at first. To strengthen or deepen the colour, just add another coat. Because of its good price, this type of paint is particularly good for painting patterns on large surfaces like floors.

Celadon
A greyish olive green used on Chinese pottery. The name may be derived from the Islamic ruler, Saladin, who had porcelain brought from China. Celadon was reputed to turn colour if it came into contact with poisoned food or drink.

Colour wheel
Isaac Newton developed the colour wheel when he was studying the effects of a beam of light shining through a prism. This splits the beam into the colours of the rainbow, and the colour wheel is the prismatic spectrum set out in circular form. It comprises 12 colours, from which all of the other identifiable hues are derived, and is based on the three primary colours: red, yellow and blue. These are pure colours and cannot be produced by mixing others. Spaced equally between these are the secondary colours: violet, green and orange (see Secondary). The other colours in the wheel are tertiaries (see Tertiary). All other colours are variations of these basics, mixed either with each other or with black or white.

Complementary colours
Each primary colour has a complementary colour which is produced by mixing the other two primaries: the complementary colour of red is therefore green (a mixture of blue and yellow), the complementary colour of blue is orange (red and yellow) and that of yellow is violet (red and blue). When equal quantities of two complementary colours are mixed they form grey. In design terms, however, the term complementary colours is generally used to refer to colours which go well together.

Contrasting colours
In technical terms, a contrast is what you get when you put a secondary colour against a primary; in common usage, however, the term has a much broader meaning and can refer, for example, to black set against white or brown against cream. Small quantities of a contrasting colour are often useful as accents in a room scheme.

Dado
This refers to the lower part of a wall which is separated by a rail known as a dado rail.

Dragging
This technique lends an expansive appearance to wall surfaces and disguises faults. An undercoat is applied and allowed to dry and is then overpainted with a glaze, generally in a lighter colour. The wet glaze is dragged, or brushed down, with a wide, dry brush, creating a softly textured surface in which fine, irregular striations give a rich, distinguished effect (see page 112).

Dye
This is a coloured powder or liquid which can change the colour of fabric which has been soaked in it. To dye something literally means to stain it or give it a new colour and in decorating the term is usually limited to fabrics but can be applied to wood floors.

Eggshell finish
Eggshell paints are generally composed of a mixture of pigments, synthetic oil (alkyd) resin and drying oils, blended to produce a very slight shine.

Emulsion
Emulsion paints (known as latex paints in the United States) are water-soluble paints made from a pigmented emulsion of a resin dispersed in water. They do not provide as resilient a surface or as rich a finish as oil (alkyd) paints, but are easy to use and are available in finishes ranging from flat to semigloss.

Enamel paints

Enamels are coatings which are applied to metallic surfaces and then fired to give a very decorative glossy finish. In decorating, however, the term is applied to paints which give a glossy, enamel-like finish to a much wider range of surfaces.

Equal tones

Successful decorating schemes are often formed from a mixture of colours of equal tones, in other words, having the same (or approximately the same) brightness, depth, lightness or dark qualities. Pastel pinks, yellows and peaches therefore look harmonious and well balanced together, as do combinations of strong bright reds, yellows and blues. In nature, the quality of the light often has the effect of reducing colours to equal tones – the pale colours of early dawn, the soft colours of dusk – while in decorating white, grey or black is often added to colours to produce a similar effect.

Freize

This is the middle division of the classical entablature (see Architrave), being the horizontal band between the cornice (above) and the architrave (below). In interior decoration, a freize may be carved, plastered or painted.

Gilding

The most common method of gilding picture frames, pelmets, pilasters, book bindings and other objects is to apply thin pieces of gold leaf to a surface, fixing it with a special adhesive. For the gilding of mirrors and ceramics, the more usual method is to apply a powdered form of gold.

Glaze

Originally, this term was applied to the glassy coating which rendered pottery and porcelain impervious to liquids. In decorating, the word glaze describes a semi-transparent, oil-based film, usually tinted with colour, which is applied over an opaque base to give a much richer effect to the surface.

Gloss paint

An oil-based (alkyd) paint which results in a smooth and shining surface, similar to the finish of a highly polished piece of furniture.

Graining

This is a method of painting which simulates the natural grain of timber.

Ground

This refers to the base on which all paints are applied and which must be properly prepared. The ground colour of a piece of porcelain is the base colour on which other designs are painted.

Harmony and harmonizing colours

Harmonious colours are those which are close to each other in warmth or coldness; for example, a harmonious monochromatic scheme (see Monochromatic) might be composed of a light tone like pearl grey, moving through middle tones such as flannel grey and ending with a deep tone like charcoal.

Hue

This is a general word for a shade of a particular colour or for any of the vast range of tints produced by mixing two of the colours in the spectrum.

Iridescent colours

The word iridescent is derived from Irides, the Greek rainbow goddess. Iridescent colours are the colours of the rainbow, forever changing and glistening, as on bubbles or mother-of-pearl.

Lacquer

In modern times, the term is applied to a coloured, opaque or clear varnish, usually on a metal or wood surface. Chinese lacquer, in which many thin layers of resin are successively applied to a surface, is a much more laborious process, though it is still used by specialists.

Latex paint

This is the US term for water-based (emulsion) paint.

Light

In decorating, there are many ways of lighting a room artificially: dimmers, table lamps, uplights, downlights, spots and so on. A change in the lighting system can create a dramatically different effect in an otherwise unaltered room, making spaces seem larger or smaller, more dramatic or gentler, at the touch of a switch. Different lights, whether natural or artificial, can also have a dramatic influence on the appearance of a colour.

Lining paper

This is a white or neutral paper, available in various thicknesses, which is used over problem walls and under new wall coverings. It is pasted up in the same way as wallpaper.

Marble, marbling

True marble is a granular crystalline limestone, though the term is used to refer to any rock of a similar appearance which will take a high polish. Marbling is the simulation of marble in paint, and has been popular since Roman times.

Matt paint

This is paint which produces a completely flat finish with no shine or lustre.

Monochromatic schemes

Monochromatic schemes are those which entail using one basic colour in a variety of shades, though they generally benefit from the addition of one or two accent colours as well as a variety of textures.

Mouldings

These are continuous decorative bands, created by making a projection or incision above or below a flat surface. They can either be very simple or ornate, such as the classical egg-and-dart or bead-and-reel mouldings.

Neutral colours

These range from black to white, taking in greys, from the palest silver to charcoal, and including off-whites and browns, from creams and camels to tans and nutmegs. Theoretically, black and white are non-colours (see Spectrum).

Oil-based paints

These paints are a mixture of oil and pigment. Synthetic resins are in fact used as the binding agent in most modern oil-based (alkyd) paints. They provide a hard, durable surface and in general have less odour than old-fashioned oil paints. They come in flat, semi-gloss or high-gloss finishes and can take many hours (overnight or longer) to dry completely.

Orange-peel effect

This paint effect is produced by dabbing one colour mixed with glaze (see Glaze) over another to give the delicately indented appearance of orange peel (see also Stippling).

Palette

This refers to the assortment of colours used

by an artist or designer for a particular picture or room scheme.

Pastels

Pastels are soft, gentle colours produced by adding a great deal of white to other colours and their many hues: for example, pink (from red); lilac (from purple), or apricot (from orange).

Pigments

The term is used for any substance which is suspended in a medium and used for colouring. Some pigments are produced from earth or clay: for example, raw Sienna, a reddish-brown clay pigment, or umber, which can be used raw or burnt to give it a reddish cast. Some are produced from stones, like malachite, which the Egyptians used to make green, or lapis lazuli, which was expensively ground down and purified to make blue in the middle ages. Others have a mineral origin: iron oxide was used for the red in the Turkomen rugs of Central Asia and the paint which early American settlers used for their barns. Many pigments are derived from animal or vegetable sources, such as Tyrian or royal purple, which the Romans made by crushing the shells of thousands of Mediterranean snails (an ounce of dye used 240,000 shells), or Lincoln green, a mixture of the yellow of dyer's broom with woad or another vegetable blue. Nowadays, many pigments are produced artificially, in other words by a chemical process. One of the earliest artificial dyes was verdigris, a greenish-blue poisonous pigment produced by the action of acetic acid on copper and popular in Roman times.

Polyurethane

Polyurethane is a varnish which is used to protect surfaces and can be applied over most decorative finishes, including wallpaper and even, on occasion, stretched fabric.

Primer

This is a coating of paint, generally white in colour, which is used to seal bare wood or plaster before the undercoat is applied.

Rag rubbing

A decorative technique of creating patterns by rubbing a rag over a wet surface first covered with a base coat and subsequently painted with a glaze in a different colour (see page 112).

Receding colours

Blue, violet and green, or colours to which these have been added, are receding colours. Known also as cold colours, they can make rooms seem larger, since they make surfaces appear to move away from the eye.

Resins

These are the binding agents – originally derived from plants but now produced artificially – which are used to give paints their adhesive properties.

Scumble

This is a common term for glaze (see Glaze).

Secondary colours

Compounds of two primary colours produce a secondary colour: red and yellow make orange, blue and red make violet and yellow and blue make green. Each secondary colour is complementary to the colour not used in its making (see Complementary colours).

Shades

These are the varying tones of any of the colours of the spectrum which are produced by adding black, grey, white or small quantities of other colours to that main colour. Blue, for example, can be mixed with white to make it pale and icy, or it can be almost black in colour. Increasing quantities of red will make it blend into violet, while the addition of small amounts of yellow will give it a greenish cast.

Solvents

These are used to dilute paints and clean brushes; for example, water for emulsion (latex) paints or white spirit (mineral spirits) for oil-based (alkyd) paints.

Spectrum

A beam of light, when shone through a glass prism, is broken up into its constituent wavelengths, represented by bands of red, orange, yellow, green, blue, indigo (violet-blue) and violet, just like a rainbow. The physicist Isaac Newton was studying this phenomenon in 1622 and it led him to develop the colour wheel (see Colour wheel). White is produced by a balanced mixture of all the colours of the spectrum while true black is a total absence of colour.

Stencilling

This is an old craft based on the repetition of a simple design (see pages 110–1).

Stippling

This is a speckled effect produced in paint on walls. In sponge stippling, a paint-soaked sponge is used to achieve the blurred, spotted effect. (See page 112.)

Tertiary colours

Colours made up of equal parts of primaries and secondaries, for example lime green, which is composed of yellow (primary) and green (secondary).

Tints

The tones of a colour which are produced by the addition of white, tints are often only marginally different from the principal colour in a scheme.

Tones

These are the gradations of a colour from its weakest intensity to its greatest; for example the range from pale pink to deep red.

Trompe l'oeil

The literal meaning of this is 'deceives the eye', and the expression is used to describe a visual deception, such as a realistic-looking window with a garden beyond, painted on a blank wall.

Undercoat

This is the layer of paint, usually white, which is applied before the chosen colour is painted on a wall.

Varnish

The name is used to describe any clear oil-based protective coating. Varnishes can be flat, semi-gloss, high gloss or, sometimes, eggshell (see also Polyurethane).

Veneer

This is a thin layer of wood laminated on top of another.

Washes

Thin coatings of paint, such as whitewash, which is a mixture of lime and water or whiting, size and water.

Wood stain

This can refer either to wood which is stained with a colour but still displays its natural grain, or to stains which have the colour of a certain wood and are applied to wood of a different kind. This latter type is generally used to make a cheaper wood look like some other expensive wood.

INDEX

ACKNOWLEDGEMENTS

Special Photography: Charlie Stebbings 1, 2–3, 10–11, 12, 13, 26–27, 28, 29, 42–43, 44, 45, 58–59, 60, 61, 76–77, 78, 79, 94–95, 96, 97.

Stylist: Victoria Whatley

The publisher thanks the following photographers and organizations for their kind permission to reproduce the photographs in this book:

Camera Press 4 below right, 40, 49 right, 57, 68, 70–71, 74–75, 82–83, 98, 104–5, 108, 109; Collier Campbell 24, 30, 40 41, 47, 90; Designers Guild 4 centre, 5, 32–3, 48, 63, 92, 106–7 (Steve Lovi) 54; Susan Griggs Agency/Michael Boys 62, 85 right, 102; Good Housekeeping (Jan Baldwin) 52–3, 70, 92–3 (David Brittain) 30–31, 51, 56, 56–57, 66, 88–89 (Malcolm Robertson) 22–23; Robert Harding Picture Library (Michael Brockway) 87 (R J Winwood) 9 centre; The World of Interiors (James Mortimer) 4 above, 15, 32, 41 (John Vaughan) 21 (Fritz von der Schulenburg) 25, 100 (James Wedge) 19, 39, 55; Options/Syndication International 67; Arthur Sanderson & Sons Ltd 17, 38, 73; Spectrum Colour Library 9 above; Jessica Strang (Design by Henrietta Green) 33; Elizabeth Whiting Associates; 4 below left, 4–5, 14, 16, 16–17, 18, 20, 23, 34, 34–35, 36, 37, 46, 49 left, 50, 52, 64, 65, 69, 72, 74, 75, 80–81, 81, 82, 83, 84, 85 left, 86–7, 89, 91, 99, 100–101, 101, 103, 105, 106; ZEFA 9 below.

The publishers would also like to thank the following companies for kindly lending fabric, wallpaper, chairs and accessories for the special photography:

Designers Guild, Bernard Thorpe, Fisch and Barker, Tulleys of Chelsea, Collier Campbell, Zoffany Ltd., Pallu and Lake, Cole and Son, John Oliver, Paper Moon, and Laura Ashley.